*The Moodys of Galveston
and Their Mansion*

❧

NUMBER THIRTEEN
Sara and John Lindsey
Series in the Arts and Humanities

The Moodys of Galveston and Their Mansion

Henry Wiencek

With a Foreword by Robert L. Moody Sr.
and an Epilogue by E. Douglas McLeod

TEXAS A&M UNIVERSITY PRESS   COLLEGE STATION

Library of Congress Cataloging-in-Publication Data

Wiencek, Henry.
    The Moodys of Galveston and their mansion / Henry Wiencek ; with a foreword by
Robert L. Moody Sr. and an epilogue by E. Douglas McLeod. — 1st ed.
        p. cm. — (Sara and John Lindsey series in the arts and humanities ; no. 13)
    Includes bibliographical references and index.
    ISBN-13: 978-1-60344-182-7 (flex : alk. paper)
    ISBN-10: 1-60344-182-4 (flex : alk. paper)
    1. Galveston (Tex.)—Biography.   2. Moody, William Lewis, 1828-1920.
3. Moody, W. L. (William Lewis), 1865–1954.   4. Northen, Mary Moody, 1892–
1986.   5. Businesspeople—Texas—Galveston—Biography.   6. Philanthropists—
Texas—Galveston—Biography.   7. Moody family—Homes and haunts—Texas—
Galveston.   8. Moody Mansion (Galveston, Tex.)   9. Architecture, Domestic—
Texas—Galveston.   10. Galveston (Tex.)—Buildings, structures, etc.   I. Title.
II. Series: Sara and John Lindsey series in the arts and humanities ; no. 13.
F394.G2W54   2010
976.4'139—dc22
2009032148

Frontispiece: Stone lion's head over the entrance of 2618 Broadway, Galveston. Tradition has it that the
stone in the gabled dormer, engraved with a "W" for Willis, was turned around by W. L. Moody Jr. to
make an "M."

Contents

Foreword

In many families, anecdotes, legends, tall tales, and stories are passed from generation to generation. Grandparents relate tales of their childhood to sleepy grandchildren at bedtime; aunts and uncles tell funny family stories around a holiday table; cousins whisper secrets as they play together. Sometimes this information is "documented" with letters, family papers, photographs, or newspaper clippings. More often, these stories are oral traditions passed from one generation to the next. Sometimes the stories have moral lessons; sometimes they record a piece of family history; sometimes they establish a family tradition.

Whatever the story, whether tall tale or documented history, these remembrances form important connections between generations.

Virginia author Henry Wiencek has done a good job of chronicling my family's history from the 1800s through the death of my Aunt Mary in 1986. Doug McLeod has done an equally good job with a short epilogue that summarizes Moody family and business happenings during the past twenty years.

My family and I are grateful to both Mr. Wiencek and Mr. McLeod for their good work. I want to convey to readers and memorialize for my children, grandchildren, and future Moody generations some additional stories and lessons that my grandfather, W. L. Moody Jr., and my aunt, Mary Elizabeth Moody Northen, shared with me and my brother Shearn and our cousins as we were growing up in Galveston, Texas.

From the time I was a small boy, my Aunt Mary told me stories of her grandfather, Colonel William Lewis Moody, who came to Texas from Chesterfield County, Virginia, in the 1850s. He prospered and provided a good life for his extended family. You will read about that trip in the first several pages of this book, but let me share with you a slightly different version of this story.

W. L. Moody left Virginia, wanting to explore the country to the west and, like many young men of his generation, make his fortune on the frontier. He traveled by boat down the Mississippi River to New Orleans. He found that city to be too hot, too humid, and too full of mosquitoes for his liking. Furthermore, he later observed that with all the bars and brothels, it was no place to raise a family. He continued to Texas, stopping briefly in Galveston. He likewise thought that city was too hot, too humid, and had too many mosquitoes.

He continued his journey on horseback, stopping for the night in Houston. Hotel rooms in those days were like office cubicles, separated by walls that did not reach the ceiling. Several guests shared a bathroom down the hall from the sleeping accommodations. Noise was easily transmitted from one hotel room to another.

During the night Great-Grandfather (and everyone else in the hotel) was awakened by a man snoring extremely loudly. His snores were always followed by the distinctive voice of one hotel guest yelling at the man to "shut up." Morning came, and the Colonel went out front, where he came upon a group of men. The voice that had yelled "shut up" so frequently during the night belonged to a man who was complaining about not having been able to sleep. The man who had snored throughout the night was standing nearby and said something acknowledging that he had been the perpetrator of the snore, offering no apology. The complainer who had gotten such a poor night's rest pulled out his gun and shot the "snoring man" dead!

Never mind the mosquitoes, heat, or humidity—the Colonel decided that Houston might be too rough a town for him, and he continued his journey north toward Dallas. He had set his destination as either the town of Fairfield or the town of Dallas, and he stopped to settle in Fairfield when his horse died.

There he formed a law partnership with an illiterate innkeeper who found young Mr. Moody's law degree from the University of Virginia most useful!

Sometimes my grandfather and my Aunt Mary told identical stories. This meant that over the years my brother Shearn and I heard the same story many times. One of our favorites was about how our great-grandfather was wounded during the Civil War. You will read about his participation in the war later in this book, but the story that Grandfather and Aunt Mary told about how he was wounded was a pretty exciting tale for young boys to hear about their great-grandfather.

Early in the Civil War the Colonel had fought, been captured, and been released as part of a prisoner exchange. He returned to battle and was then wounded. The circumstances surrounding his wounding were the meat of the tale that Grandfather and Aunt Mary related.

It seems the Colonel, along with a number of other men, was put in front of a Union firing squad, shot, and left for dead. A Christian woman who lived in the area had obtained permission from the Union Army to provide decent burials for soldiers shot by firing squads. As she was walking among the fallen soldiers, she noted that one was still alive. Instead of taking the body to be buried, she took this soldier home and nursed him back to health. He returned to Texas to complete his service.

That soldier was my great-grandfather, Colonel William Lewis Moody.

❧

The next story involves a lesson my grandfather taught me from an experience we shared. When I was thirteen or fourteen, he took me on a hunting and fishing trip with some of his business associates. I can remember my mother wondering whether this was a good idea, but Grandfather insisted.

Enoch Withers was Grandfather's chauffeur. He was also a good cook. At the end of the day Enoch prepared the group's meal, including a large bowl of chopped salad, which he made with tomatoes, celery, carrots, lettuce, onion, and cheese mixed with mayonnaise.

I was a growing boy, and I was hungry. I had eaten two or three helpings of this salad when I heard one of Grandfather's associates say, "That Bobby sure can eat!" The comment made me feel so grown up and part of the group that I continued to eat helpings four, five, and six. All the men were laughing and talking about how much I could "put away."

Quietly, my grandfather asked me to join him in the next room when I had finished eating. He said, "Come with me, I need to talk to you." When we were away from the group, he put his hand on my shoulder and said, "Son, I don't know if you realize that those men are laughing at you and not with you. They are laughing at your overindulgence. It is

Robert L. Moody Sr.,
grandson of
W. L. Moody Jr.

a wise man who does not do things in excess. Do all things in moderation."

Throughout my life I have been grateful for the good advice that my grandfather gave me as I was growing up.

Grandfather did more than give advice. He taught us lessons by letting us experience life. He did not want to hide life from us.

When I was thirteen, I had my first job at W. L. Moody and Company, Bankers. I worked there for three summers when I was home from boarding school. My mother was horrified at the job my grandfather gave me (she was my mother, loved me, and wanted to protect me). My assignment was as a runner, taking hot checks back to Postoffice Street brothels, sporting clubs, bars, restaurants, the Model Dairy, the Interurban Queen, and other businesses to collect cash for those checks that had not cleared our bank the previous day.

As I grew more experienced, I was able to represent the bank at the Galveston Clearing House and exchange checks that had not cleared our bank with runners from other financial institutions.

I worked from eight o'clock in the morning until late afternoon, often stopping to have lunch with Grandfather in the American National Insurance Company cafeteria. I treasure the opportunity he gave me to see a side of Galveston that I might not otherwise have experienced, and to spend business time with my grandfather.

When I graduated from Valley Forge Military Academy, I came home to Galveston and began attending the University of Houston. I arranged my schedule so that I could come home one afternoon a week to work with my grandfather in his office. I learned more in my time with Grandfather than any book, lecture, or reading assignment could teach me. If we take time and listen carefully to our elders, we can gain a wealth of knowledge and information.

My brother and I lost our father when we were very young, but we grew up in an extended family that included several generations—my father's sister Mary and her husband Mike Northen, my cousins, my mother, my grandmother, and most of all my grandfather. We were loved, and we learned from each of these relationships.

❧

I hope you will read these stories and this book and initiate your own effort to record your family's history for your children and for future generations.

ROBERT L. MOODY SR.
Galveston, Texas
March 2010

The Moodys of Galveston and Their Mansion

Southeast corner of the Moody mansion at 2618 Broadway.

The oak-paneled entrance hall after the restoration, providing some of the grandest effects in the house.

"Welcome Ever Smiles," proclaims the stained glass window on the main stairs.

SALVE

WELCOME EVER SMILES

(opposite page) The reception room after restoration, highly formal and refined.

The fabric on the wall in the restored library is silk damask, reproduced by Scalamandré.

In the restored living room are rocking chairs and a comfortable reading chair.

Post-restoration photograph of the dining room, with its mahogany walls and massive sideboard.

Panoramic view of Galveston dominated by One Moody Plaza, the home office of the American National Insurance Company.

(right) For the 1980s restoration work, a Texas quarry provided limestone that closely matched the original exterior limestone.

Shearn Moody Jr., grandson of W. L. Moody Jr., holds his nephew and namesake Russell Shearn Moody, 1961.

W. L. Moody IV and his grandfather, W. L. Moody Jr.

The Moody Family

꩜

I N THE ROSTER OF AMERICAN ENTREPRENEURS, there are few families whose talent for empire building exceeds that of the Moodys of Galveston. During the era between the Civil War and World War I, when many of the great American fortunes were being made, the Moodys quietly constructed a financial empire that endures to this day. They began by trading in cotton, edged into banking by extending credit to cotton growers, and then, in the early years of the twentieth century, developed an insurance company that grew to be one of the largest in the country; later they built a nationwide chain of hotels. The Moody interests survived intense competition, financial panics, national economic depressions, and natural and personal disasters, always emerging stronger than before, until by the early 1950s the family controlled one of the largest and most solid financial establishments in the country.

That empire, founded by Colonel William Lewis Moody in the 1850s, was propelled into the twentieth century by his son W. L. Moody Jr. and brought into the 1980s by the Colonel's granddaughter, Mary Moody Northen. It endures today in a variety of business and nonprofit entities still controlled by descendants of Colonel Moody—notably the American National Insurance Company, Moody National Bank, Moody Foundation, and Mary Moody Northen Endowment—and in family trusts.

As does much of Texas history, the story of the Moodys begins in Virginia. The records of Essex County, Virginia, make the first mention of

*Portrait of Colonel
W. L. Moody, age eighty,
ca. 1908.*

the name Moody in 1706, in a document relating to a land transaction.[1] The founder of the Moody dynasty in Galveston, Colonel William Lewis Moody, was born in Essex County on May 19, 1828, the eighth of thirteen children of Jameson Moody and Mary Susan Lankford Moody, who moved the family to Chesterfield County when William was two. His father died in 1842 and his mother in 1843, leaving him an orphan at age fifteen.[2]

By the 1840s opportunity for quick wealth in Virginia was limited, especially in comparison with the new western lands. Some of Virginia's finest and most energetic men and women left the Old Dominion and headed west, many for Texas. After William Moody gained a law degree from the University of Virginia in 1851, he set out for Texas via river boats and steamers, passing through New Orleans and Galveston before heading into the interior. He stopped at Houston, then just a rough frontier settlement. His plan had been to go to Dallas, but he was told the opportunities were better in the town of Fairfield, the seat of Freestone County. Family legend offers another reason for the Colonel's choice of Fairfield: his horse died there, and he could not go any farther.[3]

Upon his arrival in Fairfield, he had little in his bags but his law degree. That, however, turned out to be enough to get him started. An illiterate innkeeper who had always wanted to be a lawyer but had never had the opportunity to get an education made Moody an offer. He would be willing, he said, to provide the funds to establish Moody in a law prac-

William Lewis Moody was raised in this house in Chesterfield County, Virginia. The house was destroyed by fire in 1965.

This photograph of W. L. Moody was taken in 1851, when he was a twenty-three-year-old graduate of the University of Virginia. He would come to Texas the following year, settling in Fairfield and practicing law.

tice. Moody agreed; he later remarked that his might have been the only law firm ever in which the senior partner could neither read nor write.[4]

Freestone County enjoyed rapid growth in the 1850s. The production of cotton and cattle soared, and increased numbers of slaves were brought in from the east. Seeing the great business potential in the county, Moody brought all four of his brothers, his two sisters, and his aunt Nancy Anne to join him in Fairfield. The men founded the mercantile firm of W. L. Moody & Bros., trading all manner of merchandise in the growing county. On January 19, 1860, he married Pherabe Elizabeth Bradley, called Lizzie, whose family had come to Fairfield in 1853 from Dallas County, Alabama.[5]

Moody was an active secessionist; he did not own slaves in Texas but was financially dependent on the slave-holding cotton economy. After the outbreak of the Civil War, when Texas was arming itself, Moody

Pherabe Elizabeth Bradley was called Lizzie by her family. This photograph shows her about the time of her marriage to W. L. Moody in 1860, when she was twenty years old. Lizzie and W. L. had five children; two died as infants.

joined his friend Judge John Gregg in organizing military units. Moody himself formed Company G with Gregg's regiment, which was officially organized in November 1861 as the Texas Seventh Infantry Regiment.

Captain Moody's unit was among those defending Fort Donelson on the Cumberland River in Tennessee when it fell to Union forces on February 16, 1862. He was captured and spent several months in prisoner-of-war camps. Released in September 1862 as part of a prisoner exchange, he returned to Texas for the reorganization of his unit and was promoted to lieutenant colonel. In 1863 Colonel Moody's unit, along with the rest of Gregg's Brigade, took part in the defense of Vicksburg, the Confederate stronghold on the Mississippi River. The Texas Seventh was one of the Confederate units that attempted to halt General Ulysses S. Grant's army after it had successfully crossed the Mississippi. For his actions in the Battle of Raymond on May 12, 1863, Colonel Moody was

OPENING THE BATTLE OF RAYMOND.

SHELLING THE REBEL REAR.

HARPER'S WEEKLY.

[JUNE 13, 1863.]

THE BATTLE OF RAYMOND—REBEL CHARGE ON LOGAN'S DIVISION.—SKETCHED BY MR. THEODORE R. DAVIS.—[SEE PAGE 363.]

This engraving depicts Logan's Division battling the Confederates near Fourteen Mile Creek at the Battle of Raymond, Mississippi, on May 12, 1863. Harper's Weekly, *June 13, 1863.*

cited for bravery. He was seriously wounded in the fighting that took place around Jackson, Mississippi, after the fall of Vicksburg, and had to return to Texas. Promoted to full colonel, he was commandant of the Austin garrison and was able to be present at the birth of his first surviving child, William Lewis Moody Jr., on January 25, 1865.[6]

After the war Colonel Moody, as he was thereafter known, traveled around the state to inspect the larger towns with an eye toward resettling his family in a place with great business possibilities. After examining Austin, San Antonio, Houston, and Galveston, he chose the last because of its obvious potential as a port and as a mercantile center.

With the best harbor in the state—although not yet deep enough to accommodate oceangoing ships—Galveston had been an important town for the Texas economy since the 1830s. After the Texas Revolution, Galveston's bankers, led by the financier Samuel May Williams, kept the economy of much of the western Gulf Coast moving—although they had to operate informally because banking was illegal under the constitution of Texas. Galveston was the most important center for financing the cotton business, for trading cotton, and for handling and shipping cotton.

Cotton raised in the interior was brought to gins to have the seeds removed, was rolled into round bales, and was then transported in wagons to the coast for shipment. Because cargo space on ships was expensive, bales of cotton had to be compressed as tightly as possible. In 1842 a Galveston entrepreneur had built the city's first permanent cotton press. Shortly thereafter a steam-powered hydraulic press that could handle about 250 bales a day was built. The construction of high-density compresses required large amounts of capital, and this business was dominated by the financiers of Galveston.[7]

The Colonel moved his young family to Galveston in 1866 and entered the cotton factoring business. Factors typically received consignments of cotton from planters and sold them to representatives of textile firms, with the factor's profit coming from a percentage of the sale price. Colonel Moody also speculated in cotton. In July 1866 he established his cotton company in the Hendley Building on the northwest corner of The Strand and Twentieth Street.[8] Then, in partnership with his brother Leroy, he opened a private bank and cotton business in 1866 called W. L. & L. F. Moody. In addition, Colonel Moody briefly operated in a partnership with his wife's father and brother, Francis and George Bradley.[9]

The cotton business, fraught with risks, offered great rewards for a man with nerve, a stomach for hard bargaining, and a sixth sense for where prices would go. It was not a genteel profession. Cotton traders

It was in this house in Fairfield, Texas, that William Lewis Moody Jr. was born in 1865. Colonel Moody built the house in the year of his marriage to Pherabe. After moving to Galveston in 1866, Colonel Moody sold the house to his father-in-law. It is now known as the Bradley House.

were shrewd, hardheaded, intensely competitive, secretive, and by profession, hagglers. A trader had to have a razor-sharp mind to calculate the tiny margins of profit on each bale, to predict what New York or Liverpool might be paying for cotton several months hence, as well as to keep an eye out for any hint of drought, heavy rains, or pests. Colonel Moody established himself as one of the best traders through a combination of talent and toughness, as revealed in his business letters to his brother James. In one letter he urged James to be firm in his negotiations with a competitor: "Press Blain to the wall—settle it." In another, the Colonel warned James not to let any inside information about their business slip out: "Keep your mouth [closed] and do not let people pump your very guts out of you."[10]

The Colonel's early days in the cotton business were difficult, as he did not have much working capital. In April 1867, amid worries that there might be an economic crash, the Colonel was caught with five hundred bales on his hands as cotton prices fell. Then he had to combat a rumor that his business had been suspended. In a letter he cautions his brother about buying cotton because the price fell by three cents a pound in one day; the market was responding to rumors that Emperor Napoleon III of France was near death, an event some traders feared would cause a panic and a crash in prices. The risks of running a cotton business in Galveston were not all financial. When a yellow fever epidemic was raging in 1867, the Colonel refused to do the pragmatic thing and leave; he felt it was his duty to stay and manage his business. In a letter to one of his brothers, he said he was not afraid of death: "My mission on earth I trust is not yet fulfilled."[11]

In 1871 Colonel Moody entered into a partnership with E. S. Jemison and erected a building on The Strand in the following year at a cost of $100,000. The company sent its agents throughout the cotton-growing regions of Texas to pay cash in advance to cotton farmers for their summer crops as early as April and May. The company protected itself by shifting a great deal of the risk to the farmers, securing liens on their land—if the weather turned bad and the crop was lost, the firm took the land.

In the 1860s and 1870s the cotton market in Galveston was chaotic. Buyers were at odds with the factors, who were at odds with the farmers and gin operators. The lack of regulation in the market left the way clear for all manner of sharp practices. Farmers and inland gin operators, resentful of Galveston's control over the market, used a variety of tricks to increase the weight of their cotton bales, adding sand, rocks,

The original Moody-Jemison Building at the northwest corner of Twenty-second Street and The Strand was constructed in 1872. The building burned in January of 1882.

logs, and on at least one occasion, a corpse. Colonel Moody was one of the few men in Galveston who had the prestige and the clout to conciliate the warring factions. A brief biographical sketch of the Colonel written in the 1870s says that "in the commercial world Colonel Moody is regarded as a cool, clear-headed and able financier, and his opinions and statements have great influence." To bring some order to the market, Colonel Moody suggested in 1873 the organization of the Galveston Cotton Exchange, a group that would have authority to govern trading practices and impose regulations on the activities of traders, buyers, and handlers.[12]

In 1874 the Moody and Jemison Company opened an office in New York. The Colonel often traveled to New York for his own business and in his capacity as Texas financial agent, to which post he was named in 1874 by Governor Richard Coke. For Texas bonds sold through his New York office, the Colonel received a 15 percent commission; but sales were not easily made because the bonds did not carry a high rating. (The bustle of New York was not to his liking, however, and he decided to leave the Wall Street end of the business in Jemison's hands.) By the late 1870s the Colonel was beginning to enjoy some of the fruits of success. In 1878

Colonel W. L. Moody, photographed in New York, late nineteenth century.

he purchased a handsome three-story brick mansion at 1304 Tremont Street. One of the largest private residences in Galveston, it had previously been a hotel called the Waters House and had been used as a hospital during the Civil War.

The Colonel was a prime mover in two large transportation projects intended to aid development of Galveston. He chaired the organizing meeting of the Gulf, Colorado and Santa Fe Railroad in 1872 and sat on its permanent board. Eager to beat Houston in the competition to be the chief transportation hub in the region, the leading businessmen of Galveston were backing the railroad, which they envisioned as a link between Galveston's port and the burgeoning settlements of the

West. The Colonel also chaired the committee promoting the deepening of Galveston's harbor to accommodate larger oceangoing ships. In 1884 he testified in Washington, D.C., in favor of federal funding for the project. Despite some opposition from northern and eastern ports, which stood to lose business if Galveston's capacity were increased, as well as from some local ship-servicing companies and warehouses, funding for the project was approved in 1890. In a few years the tonnage of imports and exports handled by Galveston soared, and by the end of the century Galveston handled more cotton shipments than any other American port.[13]

The Colonel's own business suffered a setback in January 1882, when the commercial building he had erected in 1871 burned down. He described the fire in a letter to his sons Frank and W. L. Jr., then away at school in Virginia:

> Dear Boys, Our fine building is in ashes. The papers will tell you much of the sad fate. I write to say to you that none of us got injured. I came very near losing my life, however, remaining too long saving our books & was nearly suffocated & had to grope my way out in the smoke and heat. Daughter & your mother were of course

Colonel and Mrs. Moody purchased this house at 1304 Tremont in 1878. It was built in 1859 for Thomas M. League and was later the fashionable Waters Hotel. Colonel Moody lived here until his death in 1920. Mrs. Moody remained for several years but later moved to the Buccaneer Hotel. The house was torn down in 1941.

W. L. Moody Jr. at eighteen, ca. 1882.

greatly distressed but we are all resigned now. I do not lose so much in money value, but the building was an ornament to the City & I felt as you know great pride in it. . . . You see how weak it is to set our hearts on anything on earth—it may be swept away at a breath. Think of the lesson.[14]

After the fire the Colonel was chastened but not discouraged. Insurance covered much of the damage, and he set about rebuilding his business. A few weeks later he wrote a letter to W. L. Jr. expressing the need to persist in the face of difficulties: "All that is accomplished in life is by will, by effort, by patience, by perseverance—Riches will not buy wisdom."[15]

W. L. Jr. and Frank attended several preparatory schools in Virginia, and W. L. Jr. studied at Hollins College near Roanoke and at the Virginia Military Institute. The Colonel wrote his sons several letters exhorting them to do well and passing along his philosophy for success. On November 20, 1881, he wrote:

> You . . . are often discussed and talked about. Your acquaintances [are] all watching you to see what kind of material you each are & how you will turn out in life. Remember that the race is not always to the swift, etc. It takes very much to make up life. I have faith in my boys—all I desire of them is sobriety, truthfulness & honor— you all have mind & brain enough to make good & useful men— great men.

The Colonel's advice, even on such a homely matter as buying clothes, reflected his business views. "Do not get anything unless you need it—get something suitable, respectable but not costly—Exercise discretion & good sense & do not be extravagant or weak minded about what you wear." [16]

After a year of study in Germany in 1884 and 1885, W. L. Jr. enrolled at the University of Texas to study law but did not obtain a degree. In 1886, on his twenty-first birthday, W. L. Jr. joined his father's cotton firm as a junior partner. One of his tasks was to travel through the cotton region of Texas to drum up business. On one occasion young Moody lost three important new clients at a stroke when he ran up against one of his father's strong personal prejudices—the Colonel hated tobacco. W. L. Jr. ushered the three "countrymen," as he referred to planters, into his father's office to discuss bringing their business to the Moody firm. All three planters, habitual tobacco chewers, came in with their mouths full. The Colonel had forbidden smoking or chewing tobacco in his offices but was prepared to be patient in this case for the sake of his son. During the discussions the planters glanced about to find a spittoon, standard equipment in any office of the day, but there was none. They kept their mouths full as long as they could, but finally one of them stood up, went into a corner, and spat. The Colonel said nothing. Then the second planter did the same; still the Colonel kept his peace. But when the last man stood up to spit, the Colonel had had enough. He told the three planters to take their business elsewhere.[17]

W. L. Moody Jr. (left) in his Virginia Military Institute uniform, class of 1886. With him is fellow cadet Frank S. Thompson.

W. L. Jr. quickly demonstrated a genius for finance. Noting that every segment of the cotton business, from planting to shipping, depended on credit, he realized that the largest potential for profit existed not in trading cotton but in providing credit and banking services to everyone involved. He urged his father to make banking a primary pursuit among the Moody enterprises. Thus they decided to open a private bank, the

Moody Bank, which was soon merged with the National Bank of Texas, of which the Colonel was president.[18]

Early in 1889, W. L. Jr. spent some time in New York City working at the Moody and Jemison Company's banking and investment office on Wall Street. He had arrived in New York during a business downturn, making it difficult to raise capital, but he was a determined young man, and when an opportunity knocked in the most unorthodox way, he leaped at it. According to a story W. L. Jr. told a reporter in 1948, one morning when he was standing in a bank line, he recognized that the man in front of him was William Marsh Rice, the great Houston entrepreneur and banker. He watched closely as Rice passed an account book to the teller and noted that Rice was making a substantial deposit. Unobtrusively, Moody followed Rice across the street to his office, asked for an interview, and proceeded to lay a business proposition before the financier: if Rice would provide capital to the Moody company, Rice would receive a 50 percent share of the profits on that money. Impressed with the young Texan, Rice agreed to advance the company $50,000, then provided an additional $50,000, repayable on demand. But he had a test in mind for Moody.

At the opening of business a few days later he summoned W. L. Jr. and requested his money immediately. The standard deadline for repayment of demand notes was noon. Just hours after Rice made his demand, W. L. Jr. was back in his office with $100,000—he had passed Rice's test. The financier shortly offered W. L. Jr. $5 million for investment, if he would join Rice in a partnership, but because it would require quitting his father's business, W. L. declined.[19]

In this same period W. L. Jr. renewed an earlier acquaintance with a young Houston woman named Libbie Rice Shearn, the granddaughter of Charles Shearn, who had been a signer of the 1835 Goliad Declaration calling for Texas independence. The Shearns were close friends of William Marsh Rice and his family; indeed Libbie had been named after Rice's wife. W. L. Jr. struck up a passionate correspondence with her, and in a few short months they became engaged. During their courtship they wrote almost daily to each other, a habit they would continue later in life whenever they were separated.

In one of his letters he described the lot of a young man on the way up in business: "I would give anything in the world if I could go to see you, and talk with you, and ride with you, and do as other people do, but mine is a busy life and very few idle moments do I know; I have

FRANK B. MOODY.

WM. L. MOODY JR.

W. L. MOODY SR.

W. L. Moody & Co.

Bankers.

GALVESTON TEXAS

ESTABLISHED 1866

SCHARNWEBER

The girl who captured W. L. Moody Jr.'s heart, Libbie Rice Shearn, at the age of fourteen, ca. 1883. They would meet when he was twenty-four and she was twenty.

(left) Colonel Moody and his sons W. L. Jr. and Frank are pictured in an advertisement for W. L. Moody and Company, Bankers, ca. 1890.

Honeymoon photograph of W. L. Jr., Libbie, and unknown, 1890.

charge of our business here, which means I must be in the office from morning to night every day of the week except Sunday and usually half of Sunday."[20] On the day after their engagement, he wrote: "My business and ambition were once my guiding stars & I dreamed of being rich & having a great business house know[n] far & wide, but now things are changed. My soul and mind are yours, & ambitions, business, and all shall be subserved to the wishes of my sweet Sweetheart."[21]

They were married on August 26, 1890, at the First Methodist Church in Hull, Massachusetts, staying at the summer home of Libbie's sister Mary, who was married to a cousin, Charles House. After their marriage the couple moved to New York City, where W. L. Jr. resumed his work at Moody and Jemison Company. In November 1890 Frank Moody joined his brother at the New York office.[22] They kept in close touch with their father in Galveston, giving him daily market and banking reports by mail and telegraph. They telegraphed sensitive financial information in cryptograms, using a set of prearranged code words, so that messengers and telegraph operators would not become privy to information that would be of value to the Moodys' competitors. Some words beginning with the letter *A,* for example, stood for dollar amounts, and the word *colic* aptly

*Master bedroom in
W. L. Moody Jr.'s house at
2201 Avenue M, ca. 1892.
Much of the furniture
was moved in 1900 to the
family's new house at 2618
Broadway, as were other
household objects.*

*The rebuilt Moody and
Company Building at
Twenty-second and The
Strand. This was the
structure replacing the
Moody-Jemison Building
that had burned in 1882.
It remains standing today
except for the fourth floor,
which was blown off in
the 1900 Storm.*

From left: Sealy Hutchings, W. L. Moody Jr., and his brother Frank Bradley Moody,
ca. 1890. This photograph hung above the mantle in Colonel Moody's bedroom.

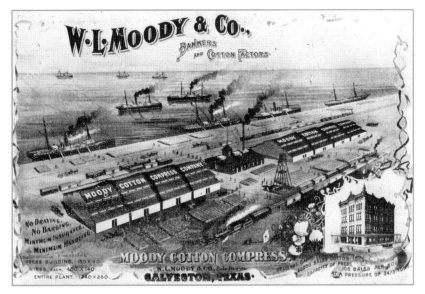

Lithograph for W. L. Moody and Company showing the cotton compress, warehouses, rail lines, wharves, and the company headquarters, late 1890s. Cotton bales were compressed into high-density bales for shipping.

Colonel Moody (far right) in the sample room at the W. L. Moody Cotton Compress.

Colonel Moody (seated second from left) with staff at the Moody Cotton Compress.

The Moody children arrived in the 1890s: Mary Elizabeth was born in 1892 (top left, showing her at age two); William Lewis III, born in 1894 (top right, age ten); Shearn, born in 1895 (bottom, about age four); and Libbie, born in 1897 (opposite page, about age two).

stood for "overdrawn." Thus, an 1891 cable saying: "Colic advent brazos cash balance Adonis all well" meant: "You are overdrawn $58,000 but credit is easily available. Our cash balance is $54,000. All well."[23]

The Moodys decided to close their New York operations in early 1891; their banking and investment operations had not worked out as well as hoped. In addition, W. L. Jr. and Libbie were eager to come home to Galveston and start a family. Colonel Moody built a house at 2201 Avenue M, behind his own home, for his son and daughter-in-law. Their first child, Mary, was born on February 10, 1892, followed by William Lewis III on January 7, 1894; Shearn on November 2, 1895; and Libbie on November 22, 1897.

Thanks in part to the deepening of its harbor, Galveston's commerce was booming. The city was handling not only the huge cotton shipments from Texas to the Northeast and to England but also dry goods and manufactured goods destined for the interior and boatloads of immigrants bound for Texas and other western states. The concentration of money in Galveston earned its main commercial street, The Strand, the nickname "the Wall Street of the Southwest." The Moodys were expanding their operations to include a new high-density cotton compress, construction of which began in 1894. When completed, it would be the most modern compress in Texas.[24]

Mary Moody and her brother William III in their bedroom at 2201 Avenue M.

The 1890s were a crucial decade for W. L. Moody Jr. Although still a young man—he turned thirty in 1895—he was beginning to take charge of the wide-ranging Moody enterprises. It was a period of turbulence in the national economy. The eastern financial markets had collapsed in the Panic of 1893, the effects of which cascaded across the country, causing banks and businesses to fail with stunning suddenness. It was not a place or time for a fainthearted businessman.

As W. L. Jr. wrote to Libbie in August 1896, "It takes a cool & steady nerve to manage properly." He was writing to her to describe a crisis on The Strand: "Finances etc. look very gloomy & the business outlook worst I have ever seen. . . . I am afraid we are on the verge of the most awful panic in the history of this country but I hope to pull through though do not expect to make much money if any."[25] Barely a week passed before there was indeed trouble: "Two heavy failures in New Orleans & the gloomy financial outlook has caused a semi panic here today & several of our . . . friends I know to be on the verge of going under today but thank goodness we are solid for the present any way."[26]

The law of survival of the fittest prevailed in the hectic cotton market.

In the summer of 1899, a firm run by friends of the Moodys, the Cleveland family of Houston, went under.[27] Despite his friendship with the unfortunate family, W. L. Jr. joined the other traders in the region in getting what he could of the wreckage, as he explained to Libbie in a letter on August 11, 1899: "I feel sorry for the Clevelands & nearly every one expresses sympathy; we will, however, gain good many new customers by it & it should mean at least 10000 bales more cotton for us: I am very busy & working hard to rope in all his customers I possibly can."[28] Just a few weeks later there was another failure that shook the Galveston community: "McCarthy & Co [cotton brokers] have just closed up & there is a good deal of excitement in town; I am doing what I can to keep our firm 'OK' & am in good shape for most anything."[29]

The possibility of a sudden crisis that could wipe out the business kept W. L. Jr. in Galveston every summer. To spare his family the discomforts of the heat and the threat of storms and disease during the hottest months of July, August, and September, he took Libbie and the children

The Pherabe *was one of the Moody family's steam yachts, ca. 1898.*

W. L. Moody Jr. on board the Pherabe *in August 1898. In the background is the Galveston Quarantine Station.*

to such fashionable resorts as Mackinac Island in Michigan; Asheville, North Carolina; Saratoga Springs, New York; and Warm Springs, Virginia. W. L. Jr., however, had inherited his father's sense of duty. After staying with his family for a couple of weeks he would return home to tend to the business, joining other "summer widowers" in Galveston. "I am not trying to have very much fun," he wrote to Libbie on August 12, 1899. "I feel very energetic & am hustling for business & to make money—I don't believe there ever was a man with more ambition than myself." As his father had done before him, he remained through a yellow fever outbreak one year, writing to Libbie: "I shall not run under almost any circumstances but will protect myself best I can & trust to the good Lord to do the balance."[30]

The summer letters of W. L. Jr. and Libbie to each other during their separations provide a vivid picture of Galveston social and business life. After a full day at the office, W. L. Jr. usually took up his other summertime duty—entertaining his father. The Colonel, then in his seventies,

The men of the family were avid duck hunters. Lake Surprise beside Galveston Bay was purchased in 1892 and was a favorite spot for relaxation and politics. Here, Colonel Moody has shot a morning's bag of waterfowl, ca. 1900.

The Moody home, ranches, and other properties played host to many of the political elite of the day. From left: Texas governor Pat Neff, W. L. Moody Jr., and three-time Democratic presidential candidate William Jennings Bryan at Lake Surprise in 1924.

enjoyed sitting at home in the evening and talking endlessly; W. L. Jr. was often at his wits' end to hold up his side of the conversation night after night. When he could get away from the Colonel, or when the Colonel was not in Galveston, he often spent an evening having dinner with friends. He also went to dinners and dances at the Garten Verein, a private park with an open-air pavilion that was one of the main gathering places in the summer. Another favorite place for socializing was Galveston's magnificent beach, where W. L. Jr. often went for a stroll or to hear concerts—"It is a regular Coney Island," he wrote. "You can see and do anything you want out there."[31] But his greatest pleasure was setting out on the family's fishing yacht for a weekend. The Colonel and W. L. Jr. were both avid fishermen and owned a succession of yachts—the one form of entertainment on which they were willing to spend any money. In 1891, when W. L. Jr. was in the New York office, his business telegrams included frequent reports on his search for a yacht for his father.

The Moodys were also avid duck hunters. In 1892 the Colonel acquired Lake Surprise on the eastern Galveston Bay spit called Smith Point, north of the Bolivar Peninsula, where they went every weekend during the hunting season. Here they often entertained business clients as well as prominent political friends, such as William Jennings Bryan and Texas governor James Hogg. Governor Hogg was a close friend of the Colonel. Both men shared the populist outlook exemplified by Bryan. Moody had actively supported the creation of the Texas Railroad Commission, which regulated the railroad and protected the interests of the state's farmers.

Forest W. McNeir, whom the Colonel hired in 1897 to manage Lake Surprise, left a lively account in his memoirs of his two years of service. He described Bryan, the "Silver Tongued Orator," as having "the finest voice I every [sic] heard. . . . Out on the lake he could talk to a man three hundred yards away in an ordinary voice and every word could be understood. . . . The dome in Bryan's mouth was high enough to put an egg in. That night at supper he put four ducks into it, eating them so fast they almost vanished like gunsmoke."[32] Governor Hogg, McNeir observed, was such a poor shot that "he couldn't have hit a hay stack, if it had been

William Jennings Bryan cutting wood at Lake Surprise.

A fit W. L. Moody Jr. adopts a boxing pose in the nursery of the house at 2201 Avenue M, ca. 1892.

moving a little." One of McNeir's co-workers provided a little surreptitious help: "Paschal sat in the skiff behind him, and every time the Governor would shoot, Paschal would shoot and kill a duck. The Governor would jump up and yell, 'Oh, boy, didn't I knock that one out!'"[33]

Serious political business was conducted during these hunting weekends. Colonel Moody was one of Bryan's major supporters in Texas; indeed, he was one of the few bankers anywhere who supported Bryan's "soft money" policy, which would foster a moderate level of inflation. Even though inflation would have a negative impact on bankers, Moody supported Bryan's stance on the currency because farmers would benefit; and the prosperity of the Moody interests depended on the prosperity of the cotton farmer. Thanks to his friendship with Colonel Moody and W. L. Jr., Bryan was able to invite important Texas politicians to Lake Surprise for dealmaking in a relaxed atmosphere. The Moodys supported Bryan's presidential bids in 1896, 1900, and 1908. Had Bryan won the election of 1896, Colonel Moody might have been offered the post of secretary of the treasury. (Mary Moody Northen and her sister

The Moody family liked to travel, especially to escape the heat of Galveston summers. Walking on the beach at Magnolia, Massachusetts, are W. L. Jr. and his daughter Mary, in June of 1900.

Seated on Bald Knob at Mountain Lake, Virginia, is Mary at age twelve, in 1905.

The Moodys embraced the motor car, purchasing their first car, a Royal Tourist, in 1907. They were photographed during an automobile tour through New York and down the Shenandoah Valley, ca. 1910. From left: Mary, Libbie, W. L. Jr., unknown, and Libbie Shearn Moody in front, with Shearn, chauffeur Lawrence Roberti, and W. L. Moody III behind.

The old hotel at Mountain Lake, Virginia. W. L. Jr. probably first saw Mountain Lake in the 1870s or 1880s when he was a student in Virginia. The Moodys spent the summer there for the first time in 1902 and vacationed nearly every summer thereafter at the resort. W. L. Moody Jr. acquired the property in the mid-1930s. The resort is still owned by the Mary Moody Northen Endowment.

Libbie Moody Thompson both had fond memories of Bryan's visits to their house, when he would take them on his lap in a rocking chair and read them stories.) Bryan remained a close friend of the family until his death in 1925, following his prosecution of the Scopes trial.[34]

W. L. Jr.'s summer letters from the 1890s mention numerous card parties and ice cream parties. One year he took up boxing; another year he bought a bicycle, which almost got him into social trouble. He invited a young widow named Mrs. Gregg to go bicycling with him one evening, but she refused, saying that she could not possibly do such a thing unless Mrs. Moody were there. W. L. Jr. innocently wrote about the episode to Libbie and got a blast in reply: "I am surprised that you asked her. I am not at all afraid of your doing anything that is wrong, but when I am away from home, I would like you to do nothing that anyone could question." Libbie thought people in Galveston "more anxious to talk than people I ever knew."[35] Gossip and rumors flew back and forth from Galveston to the various summer colonies in letters between separated spouses. W. L. Jr. relayed the case of a woman who had supposedly been "ruined" by her illicit relationships, and he wrote to Libbie about a fracas at the Garten Verein during which an angry husband punched a man who had made a remark about his wife. [36]

A constant theme of his letters is the oppressive weather. On July 21, 1897, he wrote to Libbie: "I long to see my sweet babies but I am truly thankful they are not here today for the heat since 4 o'clock this morning has been unendurable. . . . There is no breeze and the sun pores [sic] down red hot." In July of 1899 he sounded the same note: "All the life or energy has been taken out of me & I simply want a cool place to sit. I feel very well but limp & dull as a rag."[37] In such a climate there was the ever-present danger of disease. On August 1, 1899, he wrote: "I don't want you to come home until things get better here for we are having entirely too much sickness: a Doctor told me yesterday there were at least a hundred cases of typhoid fever in the city & five deaths from this alone last week; we also are having some scarlet fever & a great deal of sore throat & summer colds. The weather has gotten just red hot again."[38]

The hot spell was followed by heavy rains, which cooled the town but brought out a plague of mosquitoes. "All agree that the pests are worse than ever known before," he wrote. In the Moody offices they had to burn stink pots with repellent "to keep from being eaten up alive." In the same letter he wrote that he had obtained a new client and was doggedly carrying on: "Am working hard this year & hope to do better than last & make more money." Libbie hated their annual separations and wrote at the end of August: "I never expect to remain away again as I have this year, if we all die together by staying home."[39]

As it turned out, her offhand remark nearly came true. The following summer Libbie and the children were home in Galveston when the great hurricane of 1900 struck on Saturday, September 8. Driven by sustained winds estimated at 150 miles an hour, with gusts of over 200 mph, the waters of the Gulf rose to almost sixteen feet above sea level, demolishing about a third of the city. "Galveston became Atlantis."[40] Six to eight thousand people died in a matter of hours—the worst natural disaster in American history.

According to a family story, as the storm approached, one of W. L. Jr.'s servants went outside the house, dipped her finger into the water that was filling the street, and tasted it—the water was salty. She knew then that the street was not flooding with rainwater, which would soon subside, but that the Gulf was rising over the island. Hastily the family made their way around the corner, holding onto fences in the howling wind, to take shelter in the Colonel's large house on Tremont Street. Mary remembered that as the waters rose, she saw a cow floating by. She also remembered that the servants cut holes in the first floor so that the rising water would flow into the house and not lift it from its foundation.

Narcissa Willis, first owner of the fine house that came to be known as the Moody mansion, died in 1899.

The Moodys came through the hurricane uninjured, although the storm did heavy damage to the roof of W. L. Jr. and Libbie's home and took off the top floor of the Moody office building on The Strand.[41] When the winds abated W. L. Jr. took his family to safety on the mainland in his fishing yacht, which was then put to use in the general relief efforts. After seeing his family to the home of Libbie's brother in Houston, W. L. Jr. returned to the island, where he encountered "sights . . . never dreamed of." In a letter to Libbie he said that "sitting on our front gallery we could smell the odor of burning flesh; along the beach front yesterday I saw them burning the bodies of numbers of women, men & children . . . the wreckage and loss is beyond belief or description; one has to see it to believe it. I am so glad my precious ones are away from this hell."[42] He also reported that fifty bodies had floated in at their hunting retreat, Lake Surprise.

Olive Willis Walthew, daughter of Narcissa Willis, offered the mansion to W. L. Moody soon after the 1900 Storm.

Although many people gave up on Galveston and left permanently for the mainland, the Moodys decided to stay. The story is told that W. L. Jr. asked his father how their business could survive if many people abandoned the city, and the Colonel replied: "We both like to fish and hunt. If they do abandon the city, remember the fewer the people, the better the fishing."[43] Business activity revived with remarkable speed; just weeks after the storm, fresh shipments of cotton were arriving at the port city from the interior, and the Moody operations were as busy as ever.[44]

Moody mansion, ca. 1900. English architect William Tyndall may have been influenced by the work of Henry Hobson Richardson in the design of this house. An outbuilding can be seen to the left of it; the building on the east side was purchased and moved by W. L. Jr. in 1905. After the 1900 Storm, the decision was taken to raise the grade level of Galveston.

In 1906 the grade raising project came to Broadway and the mansion (opposite). Sections of the city were filled in with dredged sand, and the level of the island was slowly raised. Although many houses were jacked up and had fill placed underneath, the Moody mansion and some other houses on Broadway had fill placed around them. The small frame house to the left is the Quigg-Baullard cottage, which was acquired by Mary Moody Northen in 1968.

Grade Raising Scene.

Dear Binnie Nutsie was confirmed today mamma va

In the midst of the cleanup effort W. L. Jr. received a cable from Mrs. Olive Walthew, the owner of one of Galveston's finest mansions, at Broadway Boulevard and Twenty-sixth Street. The solidly built structure, like many of the other brick buildings in the city, had sustained no significant damage during the storm. Mrs. Walthew had been trying to sell the house since the death of her mother, Mrs. R. S. (Narcissa) Willis, the previous year. The Willises and the Moodys were related by marriage: Olive Walthew's late sister, Laura Willis Moody, had been married to a nephew of Colonel Moody. Earlier, W. L. Jr. had been one of several bidders, offering her the low price of $20,000, because he was not interested in putting a great deal of money into a house. In the wake of the

Library, 1905. Mrs. Moody received a box camera as a gift, and with it she recorded her house and interiors. These photographs later made restoration possible. The Chinese desk now in the room replaced the empire revival table, which was moved to the living room.

Libbie Shearn Moody and her children in the conservatory of the house, ca. 1901.

hurricane the higher bidders had all dropped out, and Mrs. Walthew's cable asked if Moody's offer still stood. At a bargain price, his offer indeed stood. W. L. Jr. asked about acquiring not only the house but also some or all of its furnishings as part of the purchase price. Libbie, who had been a guest of Mrs. Willis at the mansion at least once, may have been nervous at the prospect of having to manage the mansion—when Mrs. Willis died, Libbie had written, "I wonder who will have the house, it will require a fortune to keep it up." But the Moodys went through with the deal.[45] The precise amount of furnishings the Moodys acquired with the house is not known.

The mansion on Broadway would be the scene of numerous dances,

From left: Shearn, seven; Mary, eleven; Libbie, five; and W. L. III, nine, on the front porch of 2618 Broadway, ca. 1904.

musicales, card parties, and other entertainments, covered in detail by the Galveston press. The reporters noted "the luxurious elegance" of the house and the "atmosphere of charm reflecting the elegant hospitality of the host and hostess." In describing one party, a reporter commented on the "wide oaken hall . . . and magnificent suite of rooms on either side," and called the dining room one of the most magnificent in the city. The Moody children were approaching adolescence with social obligations of their own—Mary and her brother William served as hosts at a party for fifty of their young friends.[46]

The purchase of the mansion signaled to Galveston that the Moodys of the new generation were taking their place at the top tier of the city's

Mary attended Mrs. Olive Branch Briggs's private school. Mary is at far left in the middle row, ca. 1903.

financial and social ranks. W. L. Jr. was then only in his mid-thirties, but he was known on The Strand as a powerful figure. In 1900 when a major Galveston bank ran into an unexpected and embarrassing problem, its managers turned to the younger Moody to help them out. As W. L. Jr. reported in a letter: "The 1st National Bank's safe became jammed this morning and all their money is locked up so I have furnished them all they wanted to run their business. I feel proud to be in a position to help the weaker brethren when in distress."[47]

In cotton trading and banking, Colonel Moody had laid the foundation for the family's success. In 1905 W. L. Jr. launched an enterprise that would dwarf that achievement. The creation of that enterprise came about casually. In W. L. Jr.'s own account:

One afternoon I was standing in front of the Moody Bank . . . when three men, Messrs. Stubbs, Webb and Silva, came along and asked me if I did not wish to make some money and then proceeded to elaborate on the great fountain of wealth that would be created by virtue of an industrial life insurance company. . . . I requested a written prospectus showing me just what could be accomplished, and I never had a more beautiful work picture presented to me than the one they furnished, so I bought an old charter which had a few years to run and put in $10,000, which started the company and which amount was lost plus $18,000 more.[48]

Thus was created the American National Insurance Company—often called by its acronym, ANICO. At the beginning Moody owned the company in partnership with another Galveston entrepreneur, Isaac H. Kempner. In 1907 the Robertson Law went into effect in Texas, requiring insurance companies doing business in the state to invest some of the proceeds in Texas securities, which would be taxed by Texas. The law was intended to keep some of the money that Texas residents paid in insur-

Construction of the American National Insurance Company (ANICO) building, corner of Twenty-First and Mechanic streets, June 1, 1913.

W. L. Moody Jr. at age forty-two, 1907.

Libbie Shearn Moody at age thirty-four, ca. 1903.

Debut photographs of Mary Moody. Her debut party was held at the Moody mansion on December 12, 1911.

Mary (seated), at age nineteen, and her sister Libbie, age fourteen, were photographed in the parlor at the time of Mary's debut in 1911.

ance premiums from flowing out of the Texas economy, but it had the effect of driving out national insurance companies. ANICO and other Texas-based companies rushed to fill the void.[49] The volume of business was so great that the Moodys established a bank, the City National Bank, to handle the flow of money.

In 1908 the state insurance commissioner inspected the company's books while Kempner was away on a business trip. Upon Kempner's return W. L. Jr. told him the commissioner had demanded that more capital be invested in the company. Moody stated that he would not invest more money unless he had control of the company, and he assumed that Kempner felt the same way. The two decided that they would each offer a sealed bid for the other's interest in ANICO; the higher bidder would have the right to purchase the other's shares.[50] When the bids were unsealed, to Kempner's amazement, Moody had outbid him.

The life insurance business became W. L. Jr.'s favorite occupation, but in 1911 he was drawn into a banking crisis that ruined some of his friends and threatened to destroy the City National Bank. He described the sensational events in a series of breathless letters to Libbie beginning on August 1:

> Just a word because I am now working day & night & yesterday I . . . did not leave the office until 11:30 last night & it has all come about by a most deplorable & unfortunate occurrence which I don't want you to speak of to any one. E. H. Young ruined the Galveston Bank and [a bank official] lies at the point of death at home evidently [a suicide attempt]. . . . After a tremendous fight with the other Banks I succeeded in taking the business of the Galveston Nat over in a lump to the City Nat which was accomplished last night.[51]

Two days later he wrote that his acquisition of the Galveston National Bank's business was "working out well & I am receiving a good deal of praise and some curses." That day he had the sad duty of serving as a pallbearer at two funerals, that of the Galveston National Bank official who had committed suicide and that of a friend's young daughter who had been killed in an automobile accident on the beach. After the funerals he had to go right back to work, as the bank crisis was not over. Another Galveston National Bank official committed suicide, and panicky crowds descended on the Moody bank, demanding their deposits. Moody responded to the run in a spectacular fashion. In bushel baskets he put out a million dollars *in cash* so that all customers could plainly see that the City National Bank was solvent.

Even so, the run lasted two days, as his competitors spread rumors of weakness at his bank. As he described the scene, "the Bank was filled with excited people; we had secured bushels of money & paid them as fast as we could; turned every window into a teller's window." He actually found the crisis exhilarating: "I really enjoy the fight being made on us in some ways & I don't want you to worry about me in any way for I never felt better."[52] By Monday the crisis had passed and he savored the satisfaction of having beaten his competition: "Today it is all over & everything is quiet & people on every side are congratulating us &

telling us what a great thing we have done for the town; well, it was the greatest & most strenuous experience I ever had—Our [competitors] certainly went after us in great shape & I must congratulate them on their energy."[53]

Despite his assurances to Libbie that he was enjoying himself, another letter written in the midst of the crisis reveals the toll that his success was exacting from him: "We now have over 4 million of deposits & there are only 6 incorporated Banks in Texas with more deposits—this is in many ways very gratifying but it brings much work & many worries—many of the banks here . . . attack us in many ways & some of them would assassinate me if they could—but such is life."[54]

The 1911 summer letters between Libbie and W. L. Jr. revealed that an impending social event was also causing some anxiety for the Moodys. Mary, at age nineteen, was expecting to have her debut that winter. Since Mary's health had been fragile during the preceding year, the family was reluctant to allow the debut to proceed. But Mary was insistent, and her father was inclined to let her have her way.[55] Accordingly, the plans were

"Mike" and Mary Northen during their first year of marriage, 1916. Edwin Clyde Northen was forty-two and Mary was twenty-three when they were married on December 1, 1915. This photograph was taken on the front lawn of the mansion. W. L. Moody Jr. built a modest cottage for Mike and Mary at 2902 Broadway.

After being sent to Holton Arms School in Washington, D.C., to be "finished," Libbie Moody returned home in 1915. She met Clark W. Thompson, a marine stationed in Galveston. They were married on November 16, 1918. Clark would go on to serve in the U.S. Congress and become a successful businessman.

made for a grand celebration at the Broadway mansion. The event was scheduled for December, and the preparations were elaborate.

As it turned out, none of the young men who flocked around Mary won her special favor. She found herself attracted to a genial man nearly twenty years older than she, Edwin Clyde Northen, who was often called by the nicknames E. C. or Mike. He had arrived in Galveston in 1904 to attend the University of Texas Medical Branch, but eye problems forced him to withdraw in 1907. To support himself while he searched for a new career, he worked as a pharmacist and as night clerk at the Tremont Hotel. He befriended many actors who stayed at the hotel, frequently attended the theater, and became a popular social figure in Galveston. In 1913 he established his own insurance business. On December 1, 1915,

Mary and E. C. were married in a ceremony at the Moody mansion. Two other weddings followed Mary's in short order: W. L. Moody III married Edna W. Haden on May 17, 1916, and Libbie Moody married Clark Wallace Thompson III in Richmond, Virginia, on November 16, 1918.[56]

During World War I, W. L. III and Shearn both served in the U.S. Navy. The Moodys had close ties to the administration of President Woodrow Wilson. William Jennings Bryan, Colonel Moody's close friend, served as secretary of state until his resignation in 1915, and Colonel Edward M. House, Libbie's cousin, was Wilson's most trusted advisor. House had been instrumental in obtaining Bryan's support for Wilson when the 1912 Democratic Convention was deadlocked. After the election House recommended that W. L. Jr. be offered a senior post at the Treasury Department, a position he had to decline because of his business commitments.[57]

After 1917 the extended Moody family often gathered at their new ranch in southwest Texas, Silver Lake. As W. L. Moody IV recalled, his grandfather W. L. Jr. "went out there every April 3 and October 3 and

Colonel W. L. Moody and his wife, Pherabe, seated on the porch of their house at 1304 Tremont Street. Colonel Moody died in 1920. After the Buccaneer Hotel was built in 1929, Mrs. Moody lived there until her death in 1933.

W. L. Moody Jr., ca. 1920, seated in the living room of the "Valley View" cottage at Mountain Lake, Virginia. During the years 1914–18 he became a stockholder in the resort and built a cottage for his family.

stayed a month. My grandmother went with him, and so did Aunt Mary [Northen] and her husband, Uncle Mike. Usually some friends from Galveston would come and go during the month."[58] Covering some fifty-five thousand acres, the property stretches for twenty miles along the west fork of the Nueces River, across one of the wildest and most beautiful landscapes in Texas. Here the Moodys raised what may have been the world's largest herd of angora goats. The Silver Lake acquisition launched the family in the business of ranching—eventually W. L. Jr. owned eleven ranches in Texas, Oklahoma, West Virginia, New Mexico, and Mexico, on most of which cattle, sheep, and angora goats were raised. The Moody ranch holdings totaled almost three hundred thousand acres—among the largest ranching complexes owned by Texans.[59]

A chapter in the Moody chronicle ended on July 20, 1920, when Colonel William Lewis Moody died at the age of ninety-two. As he wished, he was buried in the old family cemetery in Chesterfield County, Virginia. Although he had left Virginia nearly seven decades earlier, he continued to have strong ties to the Old Dominion. He spent many summers in Virginia, served as secretary of the University of Virginia alumni group in Galveston, and donated some personal items from the Civil War to the White House of the Confederacy in Richmond.

The Colonel had lived to see a new generation, W. L. Jr.'s sons W. L. III and Shearn, take their places in the Moody enterprises. W. L. III was a nationally known boy wonder of finance. At the age of eighteen he was appointed by his father to the presidency of the family's American Bank and Trust Company. Far and away the youngest bank president in the country, he was the object of intense publicity, which he took as a joke— when the newspapers asked him for a photograph, he supplied one taken when he was eight. Later he struck off on his own, with spectacular success. Together with Odie Richard Seagraves, in 1923, W. L. III began to assemble a conglomerate of natural gas properties. By 1928, when W. L. III was thirty-four years old, their United Gas Company controlled some nineteen gas and fuel companies, twenty-five hundred miles of gas pipelines, and wells in Texas and Louisiana.[60] For a brief time W. L. III was even richer than his father, at least on paper. This young financial lord was as flamboyant as his father and grandfather had been modest: W. L. III flew around the country in a private airplane for his business trips and spent more lavishly than his father and grandfather ever had. He bought old master paintings that turned out to be superb investments in the long run, but in the eyes of his father, they were simply a waste of capital that might otherwise be put to work profitably.

Like many young moguls who enjoyed spectacular success in the 1920s, W. L. III had a spectacular fall when the stock market crashed. He held out for as long as he could, but pressed by creditors, he declared bankruptcy in 1933—a common practice today but in those days regarded

One of the last photographs of the brothers together with their father was taken in the living room at Christmas, 1935. W. L. Jr. (far right) shares the couch with W. L. III (middle) and Shearn, who would die in February of the next year.

W. L. Moody Jr. and Shearn, ca. 1932. This photograph hung in W. L. Jr.'s office.

as a disgrace. When Rio Bonito, his fourteen-thousand-acre ranch located near Kerrville in the Hill Country, was put on the auction block, W. L. Jr. bought it and gave it back to his son. However, the stigma of the bankruptcy caused an emotional break between father and son. W. L. Jr. never forgave his son for attaching the word *bankrupt* to the name Moody in the public mind. W. L. III withdrew to Rio Bonito. Although he rejoined the family enterprises later in the 1930s, he and his father continued to disagree over policy. The philosophical differences between the two were highlighted in letters they wrote to each other in 1939. In one of these W. L. Jr. suggested that his son had allowed enthusiasm to outrun good business judgment. "You are an optimist," W. L. Jr. wrote, but "I am a pessimist [after] many years of experience . . . propositions look fine on paper, but in actual practice never come up to expectations." He was overstating the case—most of the Moody under-

takings had been extremely successful—but the underlying sentiment
was clear: W. L. III was too venturesome for his father's taste. Oddly
enough, this letter was an echo of a letter Colonel Moody had written to
W. L. Jr. in 1900 to chide him for his eagerness in business: "I beg to cau-
tion you . . . we made money last season but about this one can so easily
be deceived." The Colonel had warned W. L. Jr. to beware of financial
"traps" and of being led "too far toward deep water—do not crave business too much."[61]

W. L. Jr.'s arguments to his son were vindicated by the excellent
health of ANICO's portfolio in the 1930s. The Wall Street crash of 1929
had little or no harmful effect on the company, thanks to W. L. Jr.'s
ultra-conservative financial strategy. Indeed, during the first years of the
Depression ANICO had the assets available to make large bond pur-
chases at a time when virtually everyone else was selling, at very low
prices. By the late 1930s ANICO had made enormous profits. Although
W. L. Jr.'s investment record was stellar, he was the first to admit that he

*Opening of the Buccaneer
Hotel, 1929.*

had made mistakes. In the early days of the oil business he had refused to invest in the company that would become Texaco; and during the Depression he declined the opportunity to buy the Plaza Hotel in New York at a very attractive price.

Shearn Moody, the younger son, was in the mold of his father. His hard-driving, hardheaded business sense won him few friends, but he showed all the signs of having the Moody talent for finding a profit. In 1916, when Shearn was twenty-one, his father made him a partner in the family's unincorporated bank. In 1925 he was made a vice president of ANICO and also started his own company, Security National Fire Insurance. Like his father, Shearn enjoyed the outdoors, but he was physically more robust than his father. He had been on the wrestling team at school, at an age when his father's health had been frail. In 1931, the year of his marriage to Frances Russell in San Diego, California, he purchased the Waco baseball franchise in the Texas League, founded the Galveston Baseball Association, and built Moody Stadium in Galveston. He was his father's right-hand man in the operation of the Moody enterprises, playing a large role in the management of the National Hotel Company, a chain of twenty-seven hotels that the Moodys put together in the 1920s and 1930s.[62]

The Moodys decided to become involved in the hotel business when they were unable to obtain a reservation at the Hotel Galvez for one of their most valued banking clients and thereby lost his account. W. L. Jr. was so annoyed at this mishap that he decided to build the Jean Lafitte Hotel in Galveston in 1927 to cater to his business clients as well as to the tourist business. In 1929 the Moodys built a second hotel in Galveston, the Buccaneer, and also began to acquire hotels in the South—including, eventually, the Galvez—many through foreclosure.[63]

The Moodys' interest in hotels brought them in contact in the early 1930s with a man who would become one of the country's most famous hotel entrepreneurs, Conrad Hilton. In the 1920s Hilton had begun to build the chain of hotels that would make him famous. Hilton Hotels, Inc., then consisted of eight properties in Texas. After the Wall Street crash in 1929, Hilton "went broke by inches," in his words, as travel and hotel occupancy greatly declined. Needing a loan of $300,000 to keep his enterprise afloat, he called on the Moodys. In his memoir Hilton described the rapidity with which the Moodys could make a large financial decision: "My business with the Moodys didn't take long. They heard me through, conversed briefly, and agreed to the loan." As security

Hilton put up all the stock in his company. Business did not improve as Hilton had hoped; the $300,000 was soon exhausted, and he had to default on the loan. The Moodys took control of Hilton Hotels, Inc., but—recognizing that the company's most valuable asset was its founder—invited Hilton to rejoin the company with a one-third owner-ship. To protect his interests, Hilton asked W. L. Jr. for a contract stating that in the event of an irreconcilable disagreement over management, the parties would split the company along its original lines and go their separate ways. Moody agreed, but the contract never arrived.[64]

Two men of forceful personality such as Shearn Moody and Conrad Hilton could not coexist long in the same organization. Shearn took a detailed interest in the operation of all the hotels and soon clashed with Hilton on a variety of matters. Sensing trouble, Hilton went to Galveston for a conference with W. L. Jr. "If I didn't agree as a businessman," Hilton later wrote of W. L. Jr., "at least I respected his honesty and loyalty." As he often did, Moody used his boat for this important business discussion. Out on the Gulf, Hilton asked about the missing contract. W. L. Jr. said Shearn did not want such a contract, and Moody intended to stand by his son's judgment. But Hilton knew that Moody was a man

Mary shares a laugh with her father in the living room, Christmas, 1935.

of his word and reminded him that he had *promised* the contract. Hilton described in his memoir what happened next: "For a minute he looked square at me and then said, 'Yup, b'gad, I did.' Next day the contract was drawn up and signed." Some further legal wrangling ensued, but in the end Hilton got three hotels back, along with a desperately needed $95,000 loan that he called his "blood transfusion."[65]

In the midst of the negotiation over the contract, Hilton questioned the business judgment of Shearn Moody, prompting W. L. Jr. to remark: "He's a smart boy, Connie. And I've got to stick by my son."[66] Indeed, it was Shearn who was expected to take over the Moody financial empire when the time came for W. L. Jr. to step aside; but that was not to be. On a midwinter trip to Chicago in 1936, Shearn refused to take an overcoat, caught a chill, and died of pneumonia just two weeks later on February 28, at the age of forty, leaving his wife with two young sons, Shearn Jr. and Robert L. Moody. After Shearn's death Mary and E. C. Northen spent a great deal of time with their two nephews, whom Mrs. Northen always regarded with special affection.

Shearn's death was a tremendous blow to W. L. Jr., who referred to Shearn not only as "my devoted son" but as "my trusted associate and protector . . . confidant and partner." W. L. III returned to take a top management position in the Moody interests, but his business philosophy continued to differ markedly from that of his father. W. L. Jr. was more convinced than ever that he could not look to his son as his successor. He turned instead to his oldest child, Mary Moody Northen. The two were very close: "We looked alike, thought alike, and felt alike," as Mrs. Northen once said. She shared her father's cautiousness and the habit of frugality—the Northens lived simply in a modest two-story brick house near her father's mansion.[67]

In 1933 Mrs. Northen's sister, Libbie Thompson, left Galveston for Washington, D.C., when her husband Clark was elected to Congress from the Galveston district. After finishing his term, he resumed his earlier activities with the U.S. Marine Corps, organizing a battalion of reserves. Called into service in 1940, he served during World War II in the South Pacific—he was the oldest officer in that theater—and in Washington, D.C., as director of the Division of Reserve Officers. In 1947 he was again elected to the House, where he would be Galveston's representative until 1967, serving on the Merchant Marine and Ways and Means committees. For her part, Libbie became one of the most prominent figures on the Washington social and political scene. After

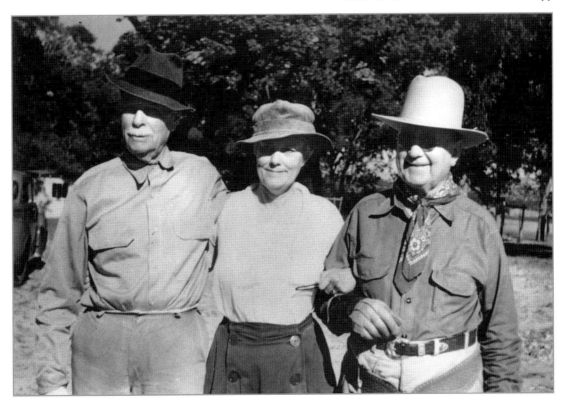

her husband's election, Libbie revived the old custom of introducing herself to the capital's elite by paying formal social calls. The Thompsons purchased a handsome mansion on Massachusetts Avenue—it had been built as the Australian Embassy—where they entertained lavishly. Their house became known as "the Texas Embassy," and Libbie soon made herself one of the capital's most popular hostesses, rivaling the legendary Perle Mesta.

By the mid-1940s Mrs. Northen was beginning to take a prominent role in the Moody businesses. W. L. Jr. discussed business affairs with her at dinner on many evenings, educating her in the intricacies of finance and corporate politics. The discussions continued into the late evening, with Mrs. Northen taking voluminous notes of her father's advice and instructions. She put her father to bed and then sat up half the night talking with her husband and writing letters; often, they would go out for ice cream in the middle of the night before returning to their own home at 2902 Broadway to sleep. The next morning Mrs. Northen would be back at the mansion to have breakfast with her father and drive with him to the office.[68] Her companionship became especially important to her father after her mother, Libbie, died in Galveston on March 24, 1943.

W. L. Moody Jr., Mary Moody Northen, and E. C. Northen at Silver Lake, their ranch near Brackettville, Texas, ca. 1950.

Like his daughter Mary, W. L. Jr. enjoyed riding. Here he is astride one of his favorite horses at Silver Lake. Written on the back of the photograph is "beauty, but not brains—proof—the 1935 flood got him."

The next generation. From left: Shearn Jr., W. L. IV, W. L. Moody Jr., Robert, and Clark Thompson IV at the new W. L. Moody and Company, Bankers building, Galveston, August 23, 1952. Mr. Moody encouraged his grandsons to follow business careers and to be the best at whatever they chose.

W. L. Moody Jr. in his office in 1950, at the age of eighty-five.

W. L. Jr. had enough confidence in his daughter to arrange positions for her on the boards of several Moody companies in the 1940s—a period of great activity for the Moody enterprises. The National Hotel Company added three major properties to its holdings: the Hotel Galvez in Galveston, the historic Menger Hotel in San Antonio, and the Hotel Washington in Washington, D.C.[69] In 1947, through the purchase of city bonds, W. L. Jr. financed the final stage of Galveston's acquisition of the wharves from his competitors, the Sealys. ANICO began a new phase of expansion in 1949 with the purchase of the Conservative Life Insurance Company and by starting to offer credit life insurance.

Although he was approaching the age of ninety, W. L. Jr. remained vigorous, continuing to preside over the management and expansion of the many Moody interests, never considering the idea of retiring. Business was his passion, and as long as he could relax on weekends on his fishing boat, he was content. As he had written many years earlier to his

Mountain Lake Hotel, ca. 1937. W. L. Moody Jr. built this stone structure to replace an earlier wooden building when he purchased the property in the mid-1930s. Mary Moody Northen spent all the time there she could. She continued to go there until her death in 1986.

Mary loved her horses. This is her favorite, Tamale, at Silver Lake Ranch, April 17, 1954.

Mary Moody Northen talking to John Rose of the National Hotel Company at a Christmas Party, 1955. A naturally shy person, Mrs. Northen had to come out of her shell to take on the responsibilities of leadership after the death of her father.

wife: "Do not worry about me for my capacity for work seems endless & really I enjoy it; it is just like playing cards and succeeding in winning."[70] After working a full day on Monday, July 19, 1954, he was stricken with pneumonia; he died two days later, on July 21.

For decades W. L. Moody Jr. had avoided public attention outside his home city—his chauffeur, Enoch Withers, remarked, "Mr. Moody *hated* publicity." He had no desire to trumpet his achievements in the press. But at his death certain information had to become public. Only then did the magnitude of his financial exploits become known: his fortune amounted to about $440 million. As this magnate of insurance, cotton, and hotels was laid to rest—with the funeral cortège stretching for sixteen blocks—the anonymity that he had so carefully cultivated was swept away in a gust of publicity. *Newsweek* called him "one of the country's wealthiest and least-known men."[71]

Equally intense was the speculation about the future of the Moody financial empire, but W. L. Jr. had taken care of that in his thorough fashion. Although he had many highly talented managers at his disposal, he put greater faith in family loyalty than in mere business competence, reflecting a conservative management philosophy. His executrix and designated successor as head of the Moody empire was his daughter Mary. She suddenly found herself one of the most powerful business figures in the nation, "the first lady of finance," head of more than fifty separate corporations throughout the country. It would not have been an easy transition under any circumstances, but for Mrs. Northen it was especially difficult and sorrowful. After her father's death the one man who could have been her confidant and supporter was her husband; but E. C. had died suddenly just seven and a half weeks before her father, in May 1954. Nevertheless, having inherited her father's tenacity, Mrs. Northen took the helm of the Moody enterprises with determination. In the words of one historian, "she proved tougher . . . than anyone suspected."[72]

The month after her father's death Mrs. Northen became the president of the American National Insurance Corporation; American Printing Company; Moody National Bank; W. L. Moody and Company, Bankers, Unincorporated; News Publishing Company (publishers of the Galveston *Daily News* and *Tribune*); and Commonwealth Life and Accident Insurance Company. She also chaired the boards of the National Hotel Company and of the thirty Affiliated National Hotels; W. L. Moody Cotton Company; Silver Lake Ranches, Inc.; and the Southern Trading Company. Although many of these positions eventually devolved upon other executives, Mrs. Northen remained active in the leadership of these firms as long as they continued to be a part of the Moody interests. Among these activities, she served as senior chair of the Moody National Bank board and board member of ANICO and the Gal-Tex Hotel Corporation.

In running the Moody businesses, she always considered what her father would have done. She was extremely reluctant to allow the sale of any asset that her father had acquired. It caused her great distress, for example, when her advisors decided to sell the two Galveston newspa-

THE MOODY FAMILY 61

Mary Moody Northen
and John Wayne. Mrs.
Northen particularly
admired "the Duke" as
well as General Douglas
MacArthur.

pers her father had bought in the 1920s, because he had specifically told
her he never wanted them sold. When some of the family's hotels were
put up for sale, she purchased one of them herself—the Mountain Lake
property in Virginia, where she spent many pleasant times with her husband and father.

To ensure that the Moody interests would remain intact after his
death, W. L. Jr. had established the Moody Foundation in 1942 and
placed under its control nearly all his holdings. The foundation would
provide support for religious, educational, scientific, and health institutions in Texas. When the foundation became active in 1960, with Mary

Moody Northen as chair, it was one of the largest in the country. She played a major role in shaping the foundation's policies, giving particular emphasis to its programs in history and historic preservation, a special love of hers. In 1964 she established the Mary Moody Northen Endowment to preserve the family home at 2618 Broadway Boulevard as a house museum dedicated not just to the Moodys and their achievements but also to showcase an important era in twentieth-century America.

Many decades earlier she had become fascinated with archeology when construction workers building a house at Silver Lake Ranch discovered the skeleton of an Apache warrior buried in a standing position. State officials surveyed other burials found in caves overlooking the lake. Mrs. Northen and her father had also found and examined Native American burial mounds at Lake Surprise. In the 1950s Mary became friends with the historian and archeologist Mary Jourdan Atkinson, who examined Moody land at Lake Surprise and proposed creating a small museum to display the artifacts found there.[73]

Mrs. Northen engaged extensively in personal philanthropy. She supported the Bay Area Boy Scout Council through her funding of the E. C. Northen Bay Area Council Center and various local scouting projects; for her generosity she was honored with the Silver Fawn Award by the scouts. An educational project that was of special interest to her was the Texas Maritime Academy, which was renamed Moody College and later became Texas A&M University at Galveston. She was also a supporter of Galveston College.

Among the many historical organizations to which Mrs. Northen belonged were the National Society of Colonial Dames of America, Daughters of the American Revolution, Daughters of the Republic of Texas, Virginia Historical Society, and Huguenot Society of South Carolina, to name a few. Her particular passion was genealogy—on their vacations, she and E. C. had often traveled to courthouses in the South to trace family records.

Her interest in her family's history in Virginia led her to focus much of her personal philanthropy on projects in that state. Among these were the Moody Alumni Hall at the Virginia Military Institute; the Museum of the Confederacy in Richmond (in memory of her grandfather and her great uncle, both Confederate veterans); the auditorium at Washington and Lee University (in memory of her uncle Frank B. Moody); a major athletic center at Hollins College in Roanoke; and the activities of the Stonewall Jackson Home in Lexington. She was a board member of VMI

(left) Mary Moody Northen was among the dignitaries at the groundbreaking ceremony for the new ANICO office building, 1973. (below) She operated the backhoe for the opening of the Mary Moody Northen Amphitheater at Galveston Island State Park, 1977.

Studio portrait of Mary Moody Northen seated at the Chinese desk in the library of her home, ca. 1970.

and of the Marine Military Academy at Harlingen, Texas. The University of Virginia and Virginia Polytechnic Institute also benefited from her philanthropy.

In Texas she was involved in major state cultural agencies as a board member. She served on the advisory board of the Texas Historical Commission from its start and was appointed to that commission by every governor from Allan Shivers to Bill Clements. She was a founder of the Texas Historical Foundation and a member of the board of the Texas Committee on the Arts and Humanities. Through her activities in state agencies and through the Moody Foundation she supported the creation of a museum at Washington-on-the-Brazos to celebrate the Republic of Texas. She also provided support for the establishment of the Mary

Moody Northen Amphitheater in Galveston and for the writing and performance of the Paul Green drama, *Lone Star*. Her other artistic activities included membership on the boards of Houston's Theatre Under the Stars and Grand Opera.

Mary's personal concern for Galveston was reflected in the Moody Foundation's support for the revitalization of the historic downtown area and the city's historical, educational, and cultural institutions. Under her direction the foundation provided funds for a new wing for the Rosenberg Library and for construction of the Moody Civic Center in Galveston. In keeping with Mrs. Northen's interest in history, the foundation acquired the abandoned Santa Fe Railroad terminal at the foot of The Strand and restored it as the Galveston Center for Transportation and Commerce, with a superb railroad museum. The building itself was renamed Shearn Moody Plaza in honor of her brother. The foundation also provided funds to the Galveston Historical Foundation for the preservation of historic sites in the city. These grants helped to save two important nineteenth-century houses, Ashton Villa and the Samuel May Williams House, and the 1877 iron sailing barque *Elissa*. To honor Mrs. Northen's efforts, the face of the new figurehead on the barque was carved in her likeness, made from a photograph taken at her debut in 1911. In gratitude for her support of the University of Texas Medical Branch at Galveston, she received the Santa Rita Award from the university. By the time of her death on August 25, 1986, Mary Moody Northen had more than left her mark on Galveston, the state of Texas, and beyond.

The name Moody has not received its due in the history of American wealth. The family's immense achievements in finance, the cotton trade, banking, insurance, and philanthropy are still not widely known. But that is the way the Moodys wanted it. In our era the creation of wealth can be made easier by first creating publicity. The Moodys, however, achieved their success by following the advice Colonel Moody gave his sons long ago: "All that is accomplished in life is by will, by effort, by patience, by perseverance—Riches will not buy wisdom."

The Moody Mansion

"WELL, LIB, we may live and die in a palace yet."
With those words, W. L. Moody Jr. announced
to his wife that he was finishing up his negotiations, by letter and telegram, with Mrs. Olive
Walthew in New York to purchase the thirty-
one-room mansion at Twenty-Sixth Street and Broadway Boulevard.[1]
Mrs. Walthew's mother, Narcissa Willis, had decided to build the house
in 1892 after the death of her husband, Richard Short Willis, a successful
dry-goods merchant. She wanted a home that would be as imposing as
the others on Broadway, the boulevard of live oaks that was the preferred
address of Galveston's elite.

Narcissa Willis was born Narcissa Worsham on August 29, 1828, in
Marengo County, Alabama. In 1835, her parents, Jeremiah and Katherine
Landrum Worsham, moved the family to Texas and settled in Montgom-
ery County. On June 15, 1847, at the age of nineteen, Narcissa married
Richard Short Willis, who had been born in Caroline County, Maryland,
in 1821. The Willises had ten children, four of whom died in infancy.

With his older brother Peter J. Willis, Richard operated a store in
Montgomery County called P. J. Willis and Brother. They prospered
and expanded their operations. In 1858 they purchased an interest in the
leading Houston commercial firm of McIllhenny and Hutchings, which
then became known as McIllhenny, Willis and Brother. During the Civil
War they opened a wholesale business. After the war the brothers settled
in Galveston, constructing a building at Twenty-fourth and The Strand
at a cost of $40,000.

After the death of Peter Willis in 1873, Richard was in sole control of their businesses. He became an important figure in Galveston, serving as president of the Galveston National Bank and the Texas Guarantee and Trust Company; a director of the Gulf, Colorado and Santa Fe Railroad; a director of the Southern Cotton Press and Manufacturing Company; and chairman of the Deep Water Committee. Willis died in 1892, leaving Narcissa in possession of a substantial inheritance that included the family home on Broadway. Not long after her husband's death, Narcissa, then in her early sixties, decided to demolish the house and erect a new one on the site. She commissioned an English architect, William H. Tyndall, who had come to Galveston in 1879; to decorate the interior, she hired the well-known New York firm of Pottier & Stymus.

Little is known about the early life and career of William H. Tyndall. No letters, diaries, or business documents of his have been found except some forty sheets of architectural drawings of the Moody mansion. There is no known photograph of him. Tyndall was born in the Midlands in 1841. Presumably he trained in England as an architect. In a *Galveston Daily News* advertisement on December 20, 1885, he states that he had been a pupil of the late Edward Pugin of England, the son of the great Victorian architect A.W. N. Pugin; but no evidence has been discovered to prove that Tyndall actually studied in Pugin's office. He may have had more experience in engineering than in residential architecture. Tyndall owned, operated, and may have designed a Turkish bathhouse in Southwark, a borough of London. In the late 1870s he emigrated to the United States, gaining employment on Avery Island in Louisiana. It is possible that Tyndall designed and oversaw the construction of a canal and a wharf for the salt works on the island. He arrived in Galveston from Louisiana aboard the ship *Cecelia* in October 1879 and was involved in designing a wharf structure for the Mallory Steamship Line.

Tyndall's name begins to appear in the Galveston press in the early 1880s. The *Galveston Daily News* of September 24, 1882, reported that Tyndall was in charge of the interior improvements of Trinity Episcopal Church and noted approvingly that he transformed the church into "one of the neatest temples of religion in the entire State. It is very difficult to transfigure at small cost an old structure, but in the case of this church, this has been effectively done."

The Galveston *City Directory* of 1882–83 lists Tyndall as an architect and superintendent with offices at 103 Tremont, between Mechanic and

WM. H. TYNDALL,

(Fellow of the American Institute of Architects.)

Speedy and Satisfactory Execution of All Contracts Made.

Best References Furnished Whenever Required.

Furnish Plans, Estimates and Superintendence of Construction for Any Style of Building, Public or Private, in Galveston or Interior of State.

Correspondence Solicited.

ARCHITECT AND SUPERINTENDENT.

OFFICE:—2107 Market Street, GALVESTON, TEXAS.

R. H. JOHN,

PROPRIETOR

GALVESTON TRUNK FACTORY

AND DEALER IN

Traveling Bags, Sample Cases, Pocket Books, Straps, Etc.

Finest Assortment in the State. No Trouble to Show Goods. We Can Please You.

TRUNKS MADE TO ORDER AND REPAIRED. FINE GOODS A SPECIALTY.

Market St. Bet. 22d and Tremont, GALVESTON, TEXAS.

ALSO PROPRIETOR OF THE

AUSTIN TRUNK FACTORY,

611 Congress Avenue, AUSTIN, TEXAS.

Market streets. The site of his offices changed over the years but always remained in the vicinity of Market and Twenty-first streets. Although it seems that Tyndall did not enjoy great financial success, he was esteemed by his professional colleagues. Along with Nicholas Clayton and Nathaniel Tobey, he was among the twenty-two charter members who organized the Texas Society of Architects in 1886. By the early 1900s Tyndall had closed his architectural practice and taken a job as a draftsman for the Army Corps of Engineers in Galveston. When he died in 1907 he was probably impoverished; his wife immediately afterward took up residence in a charity home, the Letitia Rosenberg Home for Ladies, remaining there until her death in 1920.

Tyndall or Mrs. Willis may have kept detailed records of the design and construction of the house, but with the exception of some architectural drawings, no documents have been found that chronicle the creation of the house and reveal the intentions of the architect and his client. Fortunately, a basic chronology of the construction can be pieced together from reports in Galveston newspapers. A social column published on March 10, 1893, notes that the plans for the house were being drawn up. An article on September 2, 1893, describes a fatal accident at the construction site—Richard Fealy, the masonry foreman, fell from the southwest corner arch, which gave way underneath him. Construction work continued until 1895 or early 1896. In September 1899, Mrs. Willis died while visiting her son's summer home in New Jersey, leaving a substantial estate, valued at $225,280. In her will she deeded the house and its contents to her youngest daughter, Mrs. Olive Walthew, who was then residing in New York City with her husband, Francis. (According to a local story, Mrs. Willis had built the house in an unsuccessful attempt to persuade Olive and her family to return to Galveston.)

The house was appraised at $40,000 and household property at $3,500—figures calculated for legal and tax purposes that do not indicate the true value of the house and its contents. The construction cost of the house can be estimated at between $125,000 and $150,000, a very substantial sum in an era when the annual net profit of the Galveston Wharf Company was about $48,000. (The Bishop's Palace, built for the Gresham family by Nicholas J. Clayton in the late 1880s at a cost of about

Advertisement in the 1882–83 Galveston City Directory for architect William H. Tyndall. The building shown is a stock graphic and not a structure designed by Tyndall.

$200,000, was also appraised at $40,000 in the late 1890s.) In the aftermath of the great hurricane of 1900, W. L. Moody Jr. was able to acquire the Willis house and some of its furnishings for $20,000. When the sale was announced, Mrs. Moody's cousin Edward House wired a congratulatory telegram to W. L. Jr., saying, "There is not another [house] in all of Texas to conform with it. . . . Tell Lib that I have always contended that she was the luckiest girl I know."[2]

Many of Galveston's grandest residences have been demolished, but several remain today to provide a glimpse of the grandeur of old Broadway. In addition to the Moody mansion, the most notable survivors are Open Gates, designed for the Sealy family by the New York architect Stanford White in 1889; Ashton Villa, an Italianate-style house erected in 1859 for the Brown family; and the Gresham residence, now known as the Bishop's Palace. The mansion Tyndall built was a palace departing from the aesthetic mode to which Galveston was accustomed. In contrast to the romantic festiveness of Nicholas Clayton's architecture, with its emphasis on heavy surface ornamentation, Tyndall's design for Mrs. Willis was a step forward to a more modern, plainer architecture, showing less concern with surface ornament. The tendency to surface plainness was characteristic of the 1890s, when architecture was undergoing a transition. In another respect Tyndall's design looked backward: its asymmetrical floor plan was typical of the 1870s and 1880s.

In the absence of any letters or notes by Tyndall, it is impossible to say definitely whether he looked to other buildings for inspiration; but the mansion does show some affinities with works of major architects of the day, notably Richard Morris Hunt and Henry Hobson Richardson. Tyndall might have taken some of his ideas from the trend-setting William K. Vanderbilt mansion in New York City, designed by Richard Morris Hunt, which stood at Fifth Avenue and Fifty-second Street. The Moody mansion's pyramidal roof and the arrangement of the towers and dormer window bear a resemblance to those of the Vanderbilt mansion. The front of the house is embraced by a bold, arcaded porch, reminiscent of the work of Henry Hobson Richardson. The façade of the mansion shows striking similarities to the courtyard façade of the John Jacob Glessner House in Chicago, designed by Richardson and completed in 1887, in the use of round and polygonal towers and especially in the use of prominent stone window surrounds against a plain field of brick. The Glessner house was featured in an article in February 1888 in the *Inland Architect and News Record,* a publication Tyndall may have consulted.[3]

The ornamentation of the façade has an English accent in the English Gothic plaques with oak clusters over the entrance arch and the late English Gothic lunettes over all the arches. The gable over the entrance is in the Dutch style—an element being used in England at the time by such architects as Richard Norman Shaw, who was designing massive manor houses in the Queen Anne style. Shaw liked to make use of elements from different periods and cultures in the same building, an eclecticism that apparently also appealed to Tyndall's eye.[4] Although not a groundbreaking architectural design, Tyndall's creation is grand and handsome in a restrained way as well as practical and modern in its conveniences—exactly the kind of house one would expect the Moodys to like.

Tyndall incorporated many clever mechanical features in the house, such as a one-passenger elevator, a dumbwaiter, a network of speaking tubes for summoning servants, a laundry with drying racks, combination gas and electric lighting fixtures, and up-to-date electrical and heating systems. He designed an intricate system of drains and pipes to direct rainwater into cisterns; gravity and pumps circulated it to bathrooms and the kitchen. Since well water in Galveston is brackish, an ample supply of fresh water was a luxury until the completion of a water line from the mainland in 1895.[5] To provide relief from the heat, Tyndall included

An early twentieth-century photograph of the east side of the house shows the tennis court and the beginnings of the pergola along the wall. W. L. Jr. began building the pergola in 1905.

five balconies and many walk-through windows; on the western side of the house, he designed wraparound window bays and angled some windows to catch the breeze.

Tyndall's experience in civil engineering is apparent in his innovative approach to the house's structural system. At the time, the usual technique for supporting the weight of a structure was a system of load-bearing walls that rose from the foundation to the roof. One disadvantage of this system was that the configuration of walls, and thus of rooms, had to be the same on each floor—small rooms in the basement were reflected upstairs. Similarly, if there was a large room on the first floor, there had to be a large room above it on the second floor to preserve the configuration of load-bearing walls. Tyndall broke away from this system by using cast-iron beams in certain places, one of the early uses of structural beams in the state. He was thus free to design large rooms on the first floor for entertaining, knowing that his layout of the second-floor bedrooms would not be unduly restricted. Perhaps the cleverest architectural touch can be seen on the arch that curves around the southwest corner of the porch. It is structurally impossible to make an arch curve—the stones at the top of the arch will pop out—yet at first glance Tyndall achieved the impossible. On closer inspection it is apparent that the two stones that seem to meet at the top of the arch are actually one curved stone scored at the center.

Pottier & Stymus was one of the most prominent decorating firms in the country. According to *King's Handbook of New York City*, the firm enjoyed a "world wide reputation for superior grades of furniture and wood-work . . . as well as for their artistic conceptions in interior decoration." The firm worked for the White House during Grant's administration and for such wealthy clients as Mrs. Collis P. Huntington, Thomas Edison, William Rockefeller, George Westinghouse Jr., Henry M. Flagler, and Leland Stanford.[6]

The interior Pottier & Stymus designed for Mrs. Willis reflects some of the changes in decorative thinking that were taking place in the 1890s. Like the architecture of the house, the decoration was not in the avant-garde, but it does show the beginnings of a break with the nineteenth century and a tentative embrace of the twentieth. In the second half of the nineteenth century, architecture expressed the uneasiness many people were feeling about the rapid social and economic changes brought about by industrialization. As the modern world put on an increasingly harsh face, domestic architecture attempted to offer an escape into the past. In the 1860s and 1870s, anti-modernism was expressed in Oriental, rococo, and medieval revivals; the 1890s saw the stirrings of the colonial revival, which evoked a vanished era of hand craftsmanship. In the first decades of the twentieth century, the colonial revival would be linked with the Arts and Crafts philosophy, which cherished simple but finely crafted objects, interiors, and architecture. The Pottier & Stymus design stands between two different versions of anti-modernism: the French rococo style of the parlor and the Roman revivalism seen in the dining room hark back to the taste of previous decades, while the colonial revival elements of the living room look ahead to the ascendance of the Arts and Crafts movement. The frieze on the entrance hall paneling also looks ahead, prefiguring the designs of Frank Lloyd Wright.

The wall colorings show the transition from the Victorian taste for dark colors to the modern taste for lighter hues. The second floor has an interesting palette of pale tertiary colors, such as terra-cotta, pink, buff, and mustard, well integrated to the tile and marble fireplace surrounds and wooden elements. These colors would remain popular for the next two decades, as evidenced by a book published in 1912, *Home Building and Decoration,* in which a page of color chips labeled "Good Tones for Interiors" displays buffs, tans, and olives similar in tone to the colors Pottier & Stymus chose for the second floor. The colors are darker on the first floor but not as deep and rich as the tones of previous decades. The entire palette of the Pottier & Stymus design was carefully planned to provide a visual harmony to the interior.

The changing attitudes toward furnishing are apparent in the lack of didactic paintings, prints, busts, and other art objects that had been used in the Victorian era to impart an uplifting moral tone to a household. In the late nineteenth and early twentieth centuries, furnishings and decorative objects began to reflect individual tastes and interests and became a means of self-expression. Also absent from the Moody house are the heavy drapery, tassels, and plush upholstery that had been popular previously. They were being avoided by the 1890s, partly because it was believed that plush furnishings harbored diseases but mainly because there was a new taste for sparser, less cluttered surroundings. Some chairs in the hallway with closely spaced spindles under the arms and across the back were clearly influenced by the designs of Frank Lloyd Wright.

Although W. L. Jr. may have been pleased at the idea of living in a "palace," as he wrote to his wife, he was not the kind of man who aspired to a royal style of life. The Moodys certainly had the financial means to indulge themselves but refrained from spending lavishly to furnish their mansion. As it was in business, so it was in their personal lives—they did nothing to excess. They were populist millionaires.

Colonel Moody had high regard for tradition; he gathered genealogical information, wrote a small book about the family's history, and developed the habit of saving letters, documents, and personal items. Mary Moody Northen was also devoted to the family's past. She sorted the papers that had belonged to her parents and grandparents, organizing them by date and subject matter, and saved furniture, clothing, books, periodicals, and photographs that others might have thrown away. When Mrs. Northen moved into the house after her father's death, she kept the decoration and furnishings as they were. The mansion remained much the same as it had been in the first decade of the 1900s.

She came to realize that the accumulated private papers, personal possessions, and furniture were significant not just as a record of the Moodys but as the remnants of an important era in the history of Galveston and Texas. After she established her philanthropic foundation, the Mary Moody Northen Endowment, she specified in her will that after her death the foundation should open the house as a museum.

In the last decades of her life, Mrs. Northen was so concerned with preserving the house that she was very reluctant to allow repairs, especially to the interior, unless they were absolutely necessary. When a pipe ruptured in an upstairs bathroom, she did not want it repaired because the job would require breaking through original tiles. She simply had the pipe turned off and never used that bathroom again. In 1961 Hurricane Carla did some damage that required immediate attention. The stained-glass window on the stairway was sent to Boston for repairs; some eroded detailing on the limestone of the façade was retouched; the roof was repaired; and all exterior masonry was pointed.

A series of storms in the early 1970s did significant water damage to the library and parlor. After one storm the canvas painting on the ceiling of the parlor fell off. The painting was rolled up, retouched, and put back in place. The stenciling on the canvas ceiling of the library was retouched in the mid-1970s. The house was very seriously damaged in 1983 by Hurricane Alicia, which struck while Mrs. Northen was away at the Mountain Lake Resort in Virginia. Many roof tiles were broken or blown off; water pooled on the second-floor balconies and flowed into the house, causing extensive water damage to the rooms and furnishings on the first floor. Although the rooms were dried out with fans and vacuum cleaners, it was feared that water had seeped into the electrical system, creating the possibility of fire or shock from short circuits. After viewing photographs of the damage, Mrs. Northen agreed to take up residence in another house nearby on Broadway.

In view of the extent of the damage, the time had come to begin a full restoration of the mansion. The subsequent restoration uncovered serious structural deterioration, so serious that the house might have become unsafe a few years later. The antiquated knob-and-tube electrical system was also hazardous. As it turned out, repair work would not be completed by the time of Mrs. Northen's death in 1986, and she never lived in the mansion again.

Everything was removed from the house. Possessions accumulated over eighty years were packed onto trucks (eight trailers were required) and placed in storage. Some items were sent out immediately for restoration. Before the house was emptied, a room-by-room inventory was made, documented by photographs.

Preservation Technology Group, Limited (PTG), a restoration firm from Washington, D.C., conducted preliminary survey work and began the first, most urgent phase of repairing the main roof. They removed the tiles from the roof, saving those that were unbroken. The company that had made the original tiles, Ludowici Celadon, has remained in continuous business and provided the restorers with the same type of Spanish field tile that had been used originally. As repairs to the exterior were under way, PTG took samples of most of the decorative finishes in the interior and began historical research into Tyndall, Pottier & Stymus, the Willises, and the Moodys. PTG's involvement with the project lasted until 1984.

The next phase of the restoration, beginning in 1985, was carried out by Eugene George, a professor of architecture at the University of Texas at Austin who had been resident architect at Colonial Williamsburg. George continued the historical investigations begun by PTG, focusing much of his effort on searching for information about the Willis family. George also established a philosophy for the entire restoration effort, deciding that the work would be carried out with the highest degree of historical accuracy possible. Since the quality of the restoration would depend on the skills of the workers, the Mary Moody Northen Endowment established its own general contracting company to manage the project and to provide hands-on training for a cadre of local workers. Before starting on the main house, the workers honed their skills by restoring the small house adjacent to the mansion for use as offices. These workers formed the core of the restoration crew, while specialists were hired for specific tasks requiring a high degree of skill and experience, such as paint and plaster replication and the restoration of furniture. Skilled masons were called in to perform the repairs on the exterior, where many of the original limestone windowsills and lintels had cracked. To replace them, Eugene George located a limestone quarry in Texas that had stone almost identical in colors to the original but more durable.

George had to contend with several unexpected major problems. PTG had found corrosion in the cast-iron railroad rails that Tyndall had used to support the wraparound porch, but George discovered additional corrosion in the structural iron beams inside the house. The installation of pocket doors had weakened some of the load-bearing brick walls, causing them to buckle slightly. The walls had to be reinforced with steel beams. In the course of examining the walls, George's team encountered Tyndall's intricate piping system for draining water from the roof into cisterns. Some pipes had deteriorated, causing leakage within the walls. The pipes were among the clues that led George to one of the biggest surprises in the house: a huge cistern located in the basement under the kitchen floor had been covered over and forgotten. It was still receiving water from the roof. Since the cistern was no longer needed, George had it drained, filled with sand, and covered.

In early 1988 the firm of Killis Almond, a San Antonio architect, took over the project. Almond, who had recently completed the restoration of the Grand 1894 Opera House in Galveston, continued the reconstruction of the exterior and accelerated the complex restoration of the interior decoration, an undertaking that required meticulous attention to detail. To achieve accuracy in the restoration, Killis Almond's team cooperated closely with the curatorial staff, which was responsible for the cataloging, conservation, and restoration of the Moody furniture, decorative objects, and personal possessions. The curator of the interior, Bradley Brooks, also had responsibility for the restoration or reconstruction of all fabric wall coverings. His projects were closely linked with the restoration of the painted and plastered surfaces, which were the responsibility of Almond's group. The research staff examined letters, photographs, and the surviving drawings made by Tyndall and Pottier & Stymus. They also conducted interviews with many family members, friends, former household staff, and acquaintances who had visited the house, asking about the uses of particular rooms; the types, colors, and patterns of furnishings; and events that had taken place at the house.

From their previous house, the Moodys brought furniture and their collections of fine silver, china, and decorative items. W. L. Jr.'s letters about the purchase refer to acquiring furnishings that had belonged to Mrs. Willis, but no inventory of the contents at the time of the purchase has been found. There is a tradition in the Willis family that the house was completely furnished when W. L. Jr. bought it, and that he acquired the entire contents, right down to the table settings—but this tradition cannot be correct. It is possible that many of the first-floor furnishings had belonged to Mrs. Willis, but in the absence of records and receipts, it is difficult to identify which Willis items may have been sold with the house and which items were brought by the Moodys or purchased later. Much of the furniture in the house was manufactured by the Robert Mitchell Furniture Company of Cincinnati, Ohio, a well-known furniture-making company of the time (the Greshams bought furniture for their house from the Mitchell Company). Some of the furniture bears Mitchell labels; Bradley Brooks was able to identify other Mitchell pieces from photographs and descriptions in the company's catalogues.

When the mansion opened as a museum in April 1991 it had been restored to reflect activities that may have taken place on the day and evening of Mary Moody Northen's debut party, December 12, 1911. The house was the scene of gala festivities, including a dance and a light supper, attended by some two hundred guests from many of the most important families in the city—"a very smart gathering of fashionable people," as the *Galveston Daily News* noted the next day. The orchestra was seated in the conservatory, and three rooms were cleared for dancing—the ballroom, entrance hall, and dining room. Tyndall's design, as it turned out, was admirably suited for entertaining on a sizable scale. The *Daily News* commented that "the space for the dancers was the largest of any residence in this city." The first floor was elaborately decorated with flowers, and the *Daily News* reported: "American Beauty roses, gardenias, orchids, and lilies of the valley and other rare and exotic flowers surrounded the debutante as she received the greetings of her friends."[7]

THE FIRST FLOOR

Most of the rooms intended for entertaining are on the first floor and are now open to the public. One more, not open to visitors, is a third-floor room that was designed as a theater, a traditional feature in the larger

Galveston houses. Counting the first floor rooms and the areas set up for dining on the third floor during Mary Moody Northen's debut, this house may have had the largest space for entertaining of any structure in the city in 1911.

Vestibule

The only room in the house that has its entire original finishes remaining, the vestibule was painted a muted rose and almost completely covered with stenciling. The stamped brass rosettes that are a recurring motif of the interior design are introduced here on the oak door frame, which is a light honey-amber color. The floor of the vestibule has the only true mosaic tile in the house, which features an unusually large amount of tile in colors such as mustard yellow, mottled olive-green, and pink with a crackled finish.

Entrance Hall

Muted classical design in the entrance hall, ca. 1915.

Pottier & Stymus created some of the house's grandest effects in the entrance hall, which is paneled in oak and has a beamed ceiling, stop-fluted pilasters flanking the doorways, and an oak parquet floor. The paneling is of a classical design, derived from the Doric order. The hall strikes a note of muted grandeur, portraying this as the home of a wealthy family.

Because the stairway was placed out of sight around a corner, there was increased space in the hall for furniture, enabling the Moodys to use it as a semiformal living room for family and social functions. Every year Mrs. Northen put up a Christmas tree here. The impressive fireplace at the back of the hall is ornamented with carved swags of foliage, eagles, and heraldic shields. A large leaded stained glass window above the stair landing, visible from the north end of the hall, shows a family of four dressed in the clothes of classical times, with the husband and wife extending their arms in gestures of hospitality. Below them is the motto "Welcome Ever Smiles."

Reception Room

Decorated in eighteenth-century French style, the reception room evokes a sense of grandeur and refinement. Highly formal parlors of this sort were often seen in high-style American houses of the nineteenth century. Being informal people, the Moodys seldom used the room, preferring to receive visitors in the somewhat less formal and more comfortable surroundings of the library. Nonetheless, they retained this room as a formal reception area, as a showplace that sets a romantic tone for the house—formal photographs of Mary and her sister Libbie were taken in the room. Against the background of the blue, gray-green, and gold silk lampas wall covering, the delicate rococo revival decoration and furnishings create a jewel-box effect.

The most impressive feature of the room is the ceiling painting, probably by Virgilio Tojetti, an Italian-American artist who may have had other such commissions by Pottier & Stymus. The painting shows the frolics of a group of *putti*, one on a leaf-form chariot, in a romantic, cloud-filled sky. Fine craftsmanship went into the plaster frieze around the painting—a light confection of strapwork, foliate scrolls, and clusters of acanthus. The gilded furniture in the rococo revival style was designed for effect, not for comfort. A curio cabinet displays small Florentine paintings on porcelain, figures of porcelain, family photos, and Oriental carved ivory curios typical of the 1890s. Some of these items may have been purchased by W. L. Jr. on his trip to Germany in the mid-1880s or by Colonel Moody on his trip to the Middle East in the early 1900s.

Rococo revival reception room, ca. 1905.

An early twentieth-century photograph shows the ceiling of the reception room. The ceiling collapsed after Hurricane Alicia in 1983. Early photos were used to guide restoration and reinstallation.

Library

The decoration of the library, like that of the parlor, has a strongly historical theme—in this case, the empire revival, which was inspired by a style that had been popular in the early nineteenth century. It was a formal style, in keeping with the use of this room as a place where important guests would be entertained and business could be transacted. The plaster cornice surrounding the ceiling features cast anthemia highlighted with gilding and moldings painted to simulate the mahogany wood trim of the casework. The chimney breast has Ionic columns, and the room also features palmettes, laurel wreaths, and classically garbed figures. There are rosettes of cast brass or bronze on the door and window casings and rosettes and laurel wreaths in the pattern of the textile wall covering.

In many mid-nineteenth-century houses, the library was decorated to evoke a solemn mood, the frame of mind thought proper for serious reflection. This library expresses newer thinking about the decoration and use of home libraries. Once a masculine preserve, libraries were becoming the gathering place for the whole family, a place where the women and children of the family could display photographs, personal handiwork, and items they had collected. In older libraries floor-to-ceiling cases were installed solely for the display of books; in newer home libraries,

Empire revival library, ca. 1919. A portrait of Colonel Moody has pride of place, naturally lit by the skylight.

Colonial revival living room, ca. 1919. This room was the most informal space on the first floor. Family celebrations and informal living took place in this room, originally designed as a billiard room.

the cases were chest high, leaving the tops free for the display of family photos and memorabilia.

The bay at the western side of the room forms a pleasant reading nook, and it also brought breezes into the room. A curious feature of the room is the light well, a shallow niche lit by a narrow skylight. The Moodys made this a place of honor—a portrait of Colonel William Lewis Moody, the founder of the family fortune, was displayed here.

Living Room

Tyndall designed this as a billiard room in his plans, but the Moodys used it as their living room. Less formal than the parlor or the library, this was a room where the family could relax together or individually. They always had rocking chairs here (as many as five at one time) and a comfortable reading chair. In this room hangs a portrait of William Jennings Bryan, depicted hunting ducks at Lake Surprise.

Located on the northern side of the house, the room was away from Broadway, offering the family a sense of privacy, a haven from the bustling Broadway scene. Its northern location would also have made it somewhat cooler than other rooms, being protected from the intense afternoon sun on the southern side of the house. A set of windows to the left of the fireplace brought light breezes into the room.

A dramatic Palladian arch establishes the theme of the colonial revival and dominates the room, leading the eye to the fireplace, raised on a dais at the western end of the room. With window seats on both sides, the space around the hearth is the most inviting in the house. The attractive woodwork is maple, but it was grained to look like birch. The small bathroom off the living room is the only one on this floor. At the time the mansion was built it was not unusual for houses of this size to have just one first-floor bathroom. The Ballantine House in Newark, New Jersey, built for a wealthy family in 1885, also has a single bathroom on the first floor, also located off the billiard room.

Ballroom

The decoration of this room was not complete when the Moodys bought the house; but it may have been furnished. A diary notation by Mrs. Northen's sister Libbie during a family trip to New York in 1910 says her mother and father had gone to buy an "old fashion[ed] tall mirror because we are going to have the unfinished room done." The Moodys used the ballroom for a variety of entertainments. An undated photograph shows flags, bunting, and crepe paper decorating the room, perhaps for a party. The family probably did not keep much furniture in this room but moved furniture in and out as required for various social functions. W. L. Jr. had the room redecorated and refurnished in 1946 and 1947, but he was dissatisfied with the changes. In a letter Mrs. Northen says she and her father "did not like it . . . and sent back some of the furniture [and] wish we could return the drapes and rug."[8]

Over the years some Moody children and grandchildren were married in this room. Mary and E. C. Northen were married here on December 1, 1915. A newspaper article reported that "the ball room was very artistically decorated in a profusion of Southern smilax and asparagus fern. These vined the windows and doors, and completely covered the south bay window, in which an improvised altar of white satin [was] banked with palms, ferns, mammoth white chrysanthemums, and lilies of the valley, with touches of white tulle. Pedestals held palms and ferns . . . [and] transformed it into tropical bowers. White satin pillows with the initials 'M' and 'N' were placed on the white fur rugs at the altar."[9] As Mary entered, escorted by her father, an orchestra in the conservatory played the bridal chorus from Wagner's *Lohengrin*.

Dining Room

The decorative theme of the dining room is Roman, to provide an appropriate atmosphere for lavish banquets. The false-beamed and coffered ceiling features plasterwork decoration of rosettes surrounded by winged *putti* and dolphins; below the ceiling is a painted and glazed plasterwork frieze with neoclassical urns and scrolls. From the floor to the frieze, the walls are paneled in mahogany. The parquet floor was laid in a herringbone pattern.

The plaster frieze was given three layers of color and finish. First a background color was painted on; then it was wiped or dusted with fine metal powder; then the frieze was glazed to give a shiny look. The metal powder created delicate glints through the lacquer. Above the frieze is a cast-plaster molding in an egg-and-dart pattern, the same as the molding along the false ceiling beams. The beams were made of plaster. There was a long tradition of fashioning *faux bois* (false wood) beamed ceilings, which could provide more subtle color effects than wood. After the beam was molded from plaster, it was painted with a base color that was then marked or "distressed" with scrapers, brushes, and feathers to give the plaster texture. Next, false graining was painted on, and finally the piece was lacquered.

Dining room, ca. 1919. When William Tyndall designed this room for Narcissa Willis in 1893, it was the largest dining room on the island. On the left is the butler's pantry, where food arrived via dumbwaiter from the kitchen below and was plated and served to the family and guests.

The panels in the coffers were carefully painted and glazed in a complex process. Slightly different base colors were painted on the flat background and on the relief. Over that, a glaze was wiped on and off so that it adhered thickly to the plaster in crevices and thinly to the surfaces, creating shades of light and dark and a subtle polychromatic effect, enhancing the three-dimensionality of the relief.

On the north wall, Pottier & Stymus installed a massive sideboard for the storage and display of silver, glass, and ceramics. This monumental piece, almost an architectural element, is ornamented with Ionic pilasters, acanthus carvings, and columns and is topped by a cornice at the same height as the wall paneling. Another striking element is the fireplace on the east wall, with a mantelpiece supported by a pair of columns. A plaster bas-relief on the chimneypiece shows hunters and hounds pursuing their quarry through the forest. The dining table and chairs, made by the Robert Mitchell Furniture Company, are in the colonial revival style. The other notable item of furnishing in the room is a folding Oriental screen.

Conservatory

The conservatory, where the Moodys raised a variety of plants and flowers, forms a quarter-circle outside the dining room and ballroom. Both rooms have doorways to the conservatory. Fashioned of wrought and cast iron, it has a structural cast-iron gutter that supports the section of its roof that is not attached to the main building. A frame of glazed wood covers the metal.

There is evidence that the conservatory was an afterthought: some stone elements on the side of the main building were shaved off so that the conservatory could be attached; and it is not connected to the house's main heating system. A small boiler underneath the conservatory sent heated water through the floor to a seven-pipe manifold along the curved (east) wall. One of the main features of the conservatory is a cast-iron fountain, its rim decorated with floral motifs and frogs. The conservatory is floored with mock mosaic tiles, which were scored to form patterns and then washed with a slurry that filled in the crevices, giving the appearance of mosaics. (The exterior balconies on the second and third floors also have mock mosaic tiles.) At large parties, such as Mary's debut and wedding, the conservatory provided seating space for an orchestra.

The Second Floor

In any family the furnishings of a bedroom change as children grow up; and children may choose to exchange rooms. Interviews with family members, friends, and servants indicate that the Moody children shifted from one room to another at various times. Thus the restoration of the boys' bedroom, Libbie's bedroom, the nursery, and the sewing room are based on informed speculation. However, photographs, letters, and oral tradition provide solid evidence for the furniture arrangements of the master bedroom and Mary's bedroom.

Master Bedroom Suite

The southeast corner is the traditional spot in Galveston houses for the master bedroom. The suite consists of two bedrooms connected by a dressing area with a bathroom, and another room off the master bedroom that is believed to have been Mrs. Moody's dressing and sitting room. The master bedroom features a fine set of Mitchell Company furniture, veneered in tropical hardwood of a light color, in a colonial revival design that was inspired by Federal furniture. There is also an unusual oak wardrobe in the Romanesque revival style. Made about 1890 by the Hampelmeier Furniture Manufacturing Company of Louisville, Kentucky, the wardrobe is decorated with carved, stylized acanthus leaves and has free-form hardware with a patinated copper finish. It carries the label of a Galveston retailer.

Mary occupied the suite's smaller bedroom in her teenage years, and she used this bedroom again when she moved into the house after the deaths of her husband and father. During her debut season, she decorated her room with party favors she had collected at other girls' events, and she suspended the favors to be given out at her own party—walking sticks and parasols decorated with crepe paper—from the wall fixture.

Dressing Room

Located off the master bedroom, the dressing room features a huge porcelain ceramic bathtub, located on a raised platform. During the restoration it was discovered that the word *nursery* was written on the backs of the door and window frames, suggesting that Mrs. Willis may have intended this as a bedroom for her grandchildren. Mrs. Moody may have used this room not only as a dressing room but also as a sitting room and private office, with a writing desk for her household papers.

The dresser in Mary Moody's room in 1911 was decorated with crepe paper favors from dances given by other girls having debuts that season. This is one of the few photographs of the second floor of the mansion prior to restoration.

Boys' Room

Furnished as it might have been when W. L. III and Shearn returned on vacations from military school while in their mid-teens, the boys' room was used at various times by the girls also, and during World War II, Libbie and Clark Thompson occupied this room and the adjacent one. There are three documented Mitchell pieces in the room, including a birch chiffonier veneered with curly birch. The room's woodwork is also curly birch. The taste for light-colored woods is evident here, because the birch was finished to a natural color. Earlier in the nineteenth century, the color of the wood would have been darker, either a walnut color or an even darker stain. On the walls are a plaque from the Hill School in Pennsylvania, which W. L. Moody III attended; a scene of Roman gladiators in combat with a bull and an elephant; and a lithograph of a military parade. The Moody boys had fencing epées, iron ice skates, weight-lifting clubs, chessmen, dominoes, and a souvenir pennant from Canada.

East Bedroom

The boys used the east bedroom as a playroom. In the 1940s it was used for a short time by Libbie and Clark Thompson; later it was converted into quarters for W. L. Jr.'s chauffeur. The bathroom serving this bedroom is the only one on the second floor that could also be entered from the hallway without passing through a bedroom.

Libbie's Bedroom

This room is furnished with a two-piece maple suite of furniture, a bed and dresser. The set bears the label of the Mitchell Company and appears in the company's catalogue. Other furnishings are a pair of maple chairs with cane seats, also from Mitchell, and an Egyptian revival stool of a type popular at the time. On the dresser are a sewing kit and a silvered pillbox from Gorham. A framed print of a romantic scene shows a young man in the garb of a knight kneeling before his lady, perhaps making a proposal. On a hanging shelf of bamboo are miniature chairs, one of them, just three inches high, made of glass. There is evidence that Libbie was interested in natural history and collected pickled snakes, frogs in formaldehyde, and other specimens. It is also known that both Libbie and Mary were given pyrography kits, with which they could make designs freehand or stenciled on wood with a hot iron. This room, located over the library on the western side of the home, has a wraparound window bay to catch the breezes. The window and door casings feature fluted pilasters. This is the only room on the second floor where the woodwork was painted.

Sewing Room

This room was marked on Tyndall's plans as a guest room, and the Moodys probably accommodated visitors in it occasionally. In summer the room was a breezy one; W. L. Jr. sometimes slept in it when the rest of the family was away on vacation.

The appearance of the house at the time of Mary Moody Northen's debut into society was selected as the guiding theme for the 1980s restoration so as to portray the heyday of the mansion—a time when its spacious rooms were fully employed as a setting for energetic family life and vigorous participation in Galveston's social calendar. The vision of Narcissa Willis and William Tyndall had brought the fine house into being, W. L. Moody Jr. had acquired it at a modest price while the city reeled from the shock of the 1900 storm, and it was as his children grew up that the mansion truly came into its own, humming with lively activity.

Epilogue

Galveston Island stood still the week Mary Moody Northen died on August 25, 1986. A family who had had a significant impact on the city and state for more than a century was in transition, and no one knew what to expect.

Wall Street shuddered. The value of American National Insurance Company stock rose by more than 25 percent in less than a week, a huge jump for such a conservatively managed and predictable family business. Rumors abounded that the Moodys would lose control of the company, and speculators predicted the stock value would soar.

They were wrong. Mrs. Northen's nephew, Robert L. Moody Sr., assumed a leadership role, and the family has retained control of the company that was W. L. Moody Jr.'s most notable business legacy. When American National Insurance Company celebrated its hundredth anniversary in 2005, Robert Moody was still in charge and he remains the chairman of the board at the time of writing.

Family always comes first for the Moodys of Galveston. Providing for future generations and leaving a legacy are of paramount importance. As the leadership of the family has passed from the Colonel to his son to his granddaughter and on to his great-grandson, several basic principles have guided the family in its business and philanthropy: the importance of moderation; the essential nature of a good work ethic; the responsibility of wealth; the importance of family; the love of Galveston; and the legacy of the Moody name.

Family members are schooled in the importance of carrying forward the Moody business empire for future generations. They are taught the intricacies of the family holdings and the economic and political circumstances under which their companies operate. During the two decades since his Aunt Mary's death, Robert Moody has led his family and its business empire to success imagined only by the most optimistic of financial analysts.

Mary Moody Northen was keenly aware of Robert's business acumen and his commitment to his family. The younger son of Mary's brother Shearn, who had died in 1936 at the age of forty, Robert grew up with his older brother Shearn Jr. and their mother, Frances, in a home in the Cedar Lawn neighborhood in Galveston. He attended local schools until the age of twelve, when he and Shearn were sent to Staunton Military Academy in Virginia. In 1948 he entered Valley Forge Military Academy in Wayne, Pennsylvania, where he graduated in 1953 as the highest ranking cadet in his class and cadet captain of the regimental staff.

After Valley Forge, Robert attended the University of Houston for a year before entering the U.S. Army in 1954. He returned to his native Galveston two years later to launch a career in insurance, banking, and real estate investments. In 1956, the young Mr. Moody began purchasing small insurance companies and melding them into National Western Life Insurance Company. He eventually acquired twenty-three firms and by 2008 National Western was a nearly $7 billion corporation.

Robert applied the same business skill to the development of Moody National Bank. Moody National opened its first branch office on the west end of Galveston Island in 1985, just before Mrs. Northen's death. The bank expanded to mainland Galveston County in 1991, opened a branch in Houston in 2004, and by 2008 had some two dozen offices in Brazoria, Fort Bend, Galveston, Harris, and Travis counties, with combined assets approaching $1 billion.

Ever mindful of the advice and example of his grandfather, Robert Moody has led a quiet life on his beloved Galveston Island, while leading his family in its business and philanthropic successes. American National Insurance Company boasted consolidated assets in 2008 of nearly $18 billion and $3.5 billion in stockholders' equity, compared to $750 million in assets and $75 million in equity when W. L. Moody Jr. died in 1954. Meanwhile, Gal-Tex Hotel Corporation, the family's hotel company, has expanded to include more than a dozen hotels in four states. Regent Management Services, founded in 1993, manages and operates a growing number of nursing homes in the Texas coastal region.

Robert and his wife, Ann Milroy McLeod, raised their "Brady Bunch," a blended family of eight children who are now grown with children of their own. Robert L. Moody Jr., Ross R. Moody, Russell S. Moody, Frances Ann Moody, E. Vince Matthews III, Lea McLeod Matthews, Dorethea P. Matthews, and Allan Watkins Matthews will write future chapters of the story of the Moodys of Galveston.

Robert L. Moody Sr., ca. 1965.

In the decades since Mrs. Northen's death, the Moodys of Galveston have suffered losses, celebrated successes, rejoiced in births and marriages, and mourned deaths. Mary's younger sister, Libbie Moody Thompson, died in 1990, followed by the last of the Moody siblings, W. L. Moody III, two years later. William's death marked the end of the second Texas-born generation of Moodys.

In 1996 Robert's older brother, Shearn Jr., died of heart and kidney failure at the age of sixty-three. Shearn and Robert's mother, Frances Russell Moody Newman, passed away in August of 2003 at the age of ninety-six. During this same time period, W. L. Moody IV continued his successful business career in ranching and oil, remaining active in family business enterprises well into his eighties.

A fourth generation of Texas Moodys has come of age and entered family business and philanthropy. These younger family members heeded the admonitions of their great-grandfather, W. L. Moody Jr., to preserve and expand family business and philanthropy. During the two decades from 1986 to 2006, the Moody Foundation grew to be the largest private foundation in Texas, with assets in excess of $1 billion. In recent years the foundation has focused on the development and sustainability of Moody Gardens in Galveston. Begun in 1982 under the leadership of Robert and Shearn, the first phase of Moody Gardens centered on rehabilitation for people suffering from head trauma, spinal cord injuries, and strokes.

In 1980 Robert's second son, Russell, suffered a closed head injury in a car accident. In response to the traumatic injuries suffered by his son, Robert established the Transitional Learning Community (TLC) for the rehabilitation of brain trauma patients whose injuries had been medically treated and for whom permanent hospitalization was neither necessary nor affordable. TLC has expanded to encompass several campuses with a variety of facilities that allow for rehabilitation at graduated levels, from post-trauma rehabilitation to long-term living.

Meanwhile, Moody Gardens has grown into a $400 million, nationally renowned educational facility and visitor attraction drawing more than two million guests to Galveston each year. Subsequent phased development has included an aquarium, botanical gardens, a rain forest pavilion, and an IMAX theater.

The Moody mansion itself has fulfilled Mrs. Northen's dream of serving as a museum dedicated to twentieth-century history. A new garage facility has recently been built to house and interpret the family cars (including Mrs. Northen's beloved 1934 Studebaker), and the mansion is once again filled with guests enjoying Galveston. It has become a popular venue for weddings, social events, and high-level civic functions, just as in the past. Hurricane Ike in 2008 deposited some five feet of water on the ground floor, ruining air handling, electrical, and other mechanical systems but doing little damage to the main living areas.

The Moody family story is among countless histories of Americans who began life in modest circumstances and attained wealth over the decades. To achieve such success is a marvel of the American free enterprise system, where ambition, courage, diligence, timing, and a bit of luck are tried and true ingredients for good business results. For those of our youth who find the beacon of financial opportunity irresistible, these rags-to-riches tales are inspirational. Some consider such achievements more attainable than they once were—it may be true that it has never been easier to succeed in business than now. Imagine what Colonel Moody's generation could have accomplished 150 years ago with universal access to education, instant communication, and the ease of transportation we enjoy today.

Today's optimism for our country's future is exciting. It is illustrated perfectly by the number of small businesses being started and maintained by newly arrived immigrants in the United States. Hard work and drive to get ahead are alive and well, and we must merely open our eyes to observe enviable models of accomplishment by our country's newest citizens.

Some may argue that we Americans, so blessed with abundance, have perhaps lost the zeal and ambition so apparent in our predecessors. This cannot be said of the Moody family. Notwithstanding substantial wealth, the Moodys of Galveston retain the qualities that have sustained their family through the generations. By choice, they are not and never have been content to be counted among the complacent and comfortable.

E. Douglas McLeod
Galveston, Texas
March 2010

Notes

The Moody Family

1. Moody Family Record Revised, 1954, Moody Family Papers, Mary Moody Northen Endowment, Galveston, Tex.

2. *Three Quarters of a Century of Progress, W. L. Moody Co.* (Galveston: Privately published, n.d.), 1–3; Notes from Essex County Records taken by Col. William L. Moody, 1 January 1900, Moody Family Papers.

3. Earl W. Fornell, The Moody Era in Galveston (MS), 2, Moody Family Papers.

4. *Three Quarters of a Century of Progress, W. L. Moody Co.,* 3.

5. Ibid., 5.

6. Ulysses S. Grant, *Personal Memoirs of U. S. Grant* (New York: World Publishing, 1952), 145–62; *House of Moody* (June 1933): 3.

7. Charles W. Hayes, *The Island and City of Galveston* (Austin: Jenkins Garrett Press, 1974), 713.

8. *Galveston Daily News,* 29 July 1866, 1 September 1866, 27 September 1866.

9. Col. William L. Moody to James Moody, 6 May 1867, Moody Family Papers.

10. Ibid., [n.d.] September [n.y.], 8 February [n.y.].

11. Ibid., 24 April 1867, 11 April 1867, 15 April 1867, 11 September 1867 (quote).

12. Fornell, Moody Era, 37, 40–41; Hayes, *The Island of Galveston,* 964; Thomas G. Rice Papers, Records of Foreclosure Cases, Rosenberg Library, Galveston, Tex.

13. David G. McComb, *Galveston: A History* (Austin: University of Texas Press, 1986), 51–52, 59–61.

14. Col. William L. Moody to W. L. Moody Jr. and Frank Moody, 14 January 1882, Moody Family Papers.

15. Col. William L. Moody to W. L. Moody Jr., 3 February 1882, Moody Family Papers.

16. Ibid., 20 November 1881.

17. Fornell, Moody Era, 623–24.

18. "Mr. W. L. Moody, Jr. 1865–1954," *House of Moody* (commemorative issue 1954): 5; Arthur M. Louis, "It's Moody versus Moody in the Struggle for American National," *Fortune* 83 (March 1971): 111.

19. "An Empire Builder Nears 84th Birthday," *Finance* 55 (31 December 1948): 28.

20. W. L. Moody Jr. to Libbie R. Shearn, 25 April 1890, Moody Family Papers.

21. Ibid., 8 June 1890.

22. Frank Moody to Col. William L. Moody, 1 August 1896, Moody Family Papers.

23. W. L. Moody Co., New York to W. L. Moody Co., Galveston, 12 October 1890, Moody Family Papers.

24. "Aristocrat, Soldier, Pioneer—Col. W. L. Moody," *House of Moody* (June 1933): 2.

25. W. L. Moody Jr. to Libbie R. Moody, 1 August 1896, Moody Family Papers.

26. Ibid., 8 August 1896.

27. Ibid., 10 July 1899.

28. Ibid., 11 August 1899.

29. Ibid., 1 September 1899.

30. Ibid., 29 July 1905.

31. Ibid., 27 July 1900.

32. Forest W. McNeir, *Forest McNeir of Texas* (San Antonio: Naylor, 1956), 77–78.

33. Ibid., 77.

34. J. S. Hogg to William Jennings Bryan, 23 May 1896, William Jennings Bryan Papers, Library of Congress, Washington, D.C.; Fornell, Moody Era, 348.

35. Libbie R. Moody to W. L. Moody Jr., 2 August 1897, 23 July 1900, Moody Family Papers.

36. W. L. Moody Jr. to Libbie R. Moody, 1 August 1896, Moody Family Papers.

37. Ibid., 22 July 1899.

38. Ibid., 1 August 1899.

39. Ibid., 5 August 1899; Libbie R. Moody to W. L. Moody Jr., 23 August 1899, Moody Family Papers.

40. Erik Larson, *Isaac's Storm* (New York: Crown Publishers, 1999), 198.

41. W. L. Moody Jr. to Libbie R. Moody, 26 September 1900, Moody Family Papers.

42. Ibid., 17 September 1900.

43. John Edward Weems, *A Weekend in September* (New York: Henry Holt, 1957), 157.

44. W. L. Moody Jr. to Libbie R. Moody, 27 September 1900, Moody Family Papers.

45. Ibid., 20 September 1900; Libbie R. Moody to W. L. Jr., 10 September 1899, Moody Family Papers.

46. Libbie R. Moody Scrapbook, Moody Family Papers.

47. W. L. Moody Jr. to Libbie R. Moody, 28 July 1900, Moody Family Papers.

48. Fornell, Moody Era, 632.

49. Alice Chambers Wygant, *Yours for Life: The Story of American National Insurance Company's First 100 Years* (Galveston: ANICO, 2005), 103–104.

50. Ibid., 106–107.

51. W. L. Moody Jr. to Libbie R. Moody, 1 August 1911, Moody Family Papers.

52. Ibid., 2 August 1911, 5 August 1911, 7 August 1911.

53. Ibid., 7 August 1911.

54. Ibid., 6 August 1911.

55. Ibid., 4 September 1911, 5 September 1911, 6 September 1911.

56. Fornell, Moody Era, 687.

57. Charles L. Mee Jr. *The End of Order* (New York: E. P. Dutton, 1980), 91; "Wilson, Woodrow," *The Columbia Encyclopedia,* 6th ed. (New York: Columbia University Press, 2007), www.bartleby.com/65/ (accessed 24 February 2008).

58. Wygant, *Yours for Life,* 57.

59. Fornell, Moody Era, 596, 602.

60. "Young Man Building New and Greater Natural Gas Industry," *Natural Gas,* 9 (November 1928): 8–9.

61. Louis, "It's Moody versus Moody," 111; W. L. Moody Jr. to W. L. Moody III, 27 October 1939; Col. William L. Moody to William L. Moody Jr., 9 August 1900, Moody Family Papers.

62. Louis, "It's Moody versus Moody," 112; Sam B. Graham, ed., *Galveston Community Book* (Galveston: Cawston, 1945), 432; Fornell, Moody Era, 654.

63. Fornell, Moody Era, 652–54.

64. Conrad Hilton, *Be My Guest* (Englewood, N.J.: Prentice-Hall, 1957), 153, 155, 160.

65. Ibid., 163, 170, 172.

66. Ibid., 163.

67. W. L. Moody Jr. to Robert and Shearn Moody Jr., 3 April 1936, Moody Family Papers; Louis, "It's Moody versus Moody," 112.

68. "Dedication," *House of Moody* (April 1943): 3.

69. Fornell, Moody Era, 643–44, 662.

70. W. L. Moody Jr. to Libbie R. Moody, 17 August 1911.

71. *House of Moody* (commemorative issue 1954): 11; "Moody's New Queen," *Newsweek* 44 (6 September 1954): 63.

72. "Mrs. Mary Moody Northen Becomes First Lady of Finance," *House of Moody* (August 1954): 3; McComb, *Galveston,* 173.

73. Fornell, Moody Era, 598–99; Mary J. Atkinson to Mary Moody Northen, 6 February 1956, Moody Family Papers.

The Moody Mansion

1. W. L. Jr. to Libbie S. Moody, 26 September 1900, Moody Family Papers.

2. Edward House to W. L. Jr., 4 October 1900, Moody Family Papers.

3. Thomas C. Hubka, "H. H. Richardson's Glessner House," *Winterthur Portfolio* (Winter 1989): 209, n. 1.

4. Clive Aslet, *The Last Country Houses* (New Haven: Yale University Press, 1982), 120.

5. McComb, *Galveston,* 103.

6. David A. Hanks, "Pottier & Stymus Mfg. Co.," *Art and Antiques* (October 1982): 84–88.

7. *Galveston Daily News,* 13 December 1911.

8. Mary Moody Northen to Janet Brown, 5 May 1947, Moody Family Papers.

9. Undated newspaper clipping.

Bibliography

ARCHIVES

Galveston Daily News (microfilm, hard copy). Rosenberg Library, Galveston, Tex.
William Jennings Bryan Papers. Library of Congress, Washington, D.C.
Moody Family Papers. Mary Northen Endowment, Galveston, Tex.
Thomas G. Rice Papers. Rosenberg Library, Galveston, Tex.

PUBLISHED SOURCES

"An Empire Builder Nears 84th Birthday." *Finance* 55 (31 December 1948): 27–28, 40.
"Aristocrat, Soldier, Pioneer—Col. W. L. Moody." *House of Moody* (June 1933): 2–4.
Aslet, Clive. *The Last Country Houses.* New Haven: Yale University Press, 1982.
"Dedication." *House of Moody* (April 1943): 3.
Graham, Sam B., ed. *Galveston Community Book.* Galveston: Cawston, 1945.
Grant, Ulysses S. *Personal Memoirs of U. S. Grant.* New York: World Publishing, 1952.
Hanks, David A. "Pottier & Stymus Mfg. Co." *Art and Antiques* (October 1982): 84–88.
Hayes, Charles W. *The Island and City of Galveston.* Austin: Jenkins Garrett Press, 1974.
Hilton, Conrad. *Be My Guest.* Englewood, N.J.: Prentice-Hall, 1957.
Hubka, Thomas C. "H. H. Richardson's Glessner House." *Winterthur Portfolio* (Winter 1989): 209–29.
Larson, Erik. *Isaac's Storm.* New York: Crown Publishers, 1999.
Louis, Arthur M. "It's Moody versus Moody in the Struggle for American National." *Fortune* 83 (March 1971): 109–12, 156–60.
McComb, David G. *Galveston: A History.* Austin: University of Texas Press, 1986.
McNeir, Forest W. *Forest McNeir of Texas.* San Antonio: Naylor, 1956.
Mee, Charles L. Jr. *The End of Order.* New York: E. P. Dutton, 1980.
"Moody's New Queen." *Newsweek* 44 (6 September 1954): 63.
"Mr. W. L. Moody, Jr. 1865–1954." *House of Moody* (commemorative issue 1954): 1–44.
"Mrs. Mary Moody Northen Becomes First Lady of Finance." *House of Moody* (August 1954): 3–4.
Three Quarters of a Century of Progress, W. L. Moody Co. Galveston: Privately published, n.d.
Weems, John Edward. *A Weekend in September.* New York: Henry Holt, 1957.
"Wilson, Woodrow." *The Columbia Encyclopedia,* 6th ed. New York: Columbia University Press, 2007, www.bartleby.com/65/.

Wygant, Alice Chambers. *Yours for Life: The Story of American National Insurance Company's First 100 Years.* Galveston: ANICO, 2005.

"Young Man Building New and Greater Natural Gas Industry. " *Natural Gas* 9 (November 1928): 8–9.

Index

About the Author

HENRY WIENCEK is the author of numerous books, including *The Hairstons: An American Family in Black and White*, which won the National Book Critics' Circle Award in Biography in 1999, and *An Imperfect God: George Washington, His Slaves, and the Creation of America*, which won the *Los Angeles Times* Book Prize in History and the Best Book Award from the Society for Historians of the Early American Republic. He has been awarded fellowships at the Virginia Foundation for the Humanities, the International Center for Jefferson Studies at Monticello, and the C. V. Starr Center for the Study of the American Experience at Washington College. In 2008 he was chosen to be the inaugural Patrick Henry Fellow at the Starr Center.